"In her alert and disarming *Little Seed*, Wei Tchou plunges us into a piercing story of immigration, family, and the search for belonging. Intertwined with this story is a devout fascination with ferns. By looking at ferns closely and with great humility and humor, Tchou uncovers larger, wilder truths about identity and connection. A suspenseful and profound heart-stopper."

—JOHN D'AGATA, author of *The Lifespan of a Fact*

LITTLE SEED

LITTLE SEED

WEI TCHOU

DEEP
VELLUM
Dallas, Texas

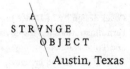
A
STRANGE
OBJECT
Austin, Texas

Published by A Strange Object, an imprint of Deep Vellum

Deep Vellum is a 501(c)(3) nonprofit literary arts organization founded
in 2013 with the mission to bring the world into conversation through
literature.

Library of Congress Cataloging-in-Publication Data

Names: Tchou, Wei, author.
Title: Little seed / Wei Tchou.
Description: Dallas, Texas : Deep Vellum ; Austin, Texas : A Strange Object,
    2024.
Identifiers: LCCN 2023042655 (print) | LCCN 2023042656 (ebook) |
    ISBN 9781646053360 (paperback) | ISBN 9781646053407 (ebook)
Subjects: LCSH: Tchou, Wei—Family. | Women—United States—
    Biography. | Ferns.
Classification: LCC CT275 .T35945 2024 (print) | LCC CT275 (ebook) |
    DDC 920.720973—dc23/eng/20231116
LC record available at https://lccn.loc.gov/2023042655
LC ebook record available at https://lccn.loc.gov/2023042656

Cover design by In-House International
Fern illustrations (on the cover and throughout the text) by Emma Hunsinger
and Tillie Walden
Interior design and layout by Amber Morena

Printed in Canada

For love

I only now understand why it is that people lie about their past, why they say they are one thing other than the thing they really are, why they invent a self that bears no resemblance to who they really are, why anyone would want to feel as if he or she belongs to nothing, comes from no one, just fell out of the sky, whole.

—JAMAICA KINCAID, *MY BROTHER*

LITTLE SEED

I. FORMATION

desk fern

CHAPTER 1 \\\\

AT THE TIME OF MY BROTHER'S first psychotic break, I knew nothing about ferns but that I had one and it was dying. I watched its seashell leaves wilt. They were jade, then chartreuse, then cream and sienna, like a stained pillowcase. I couldn't let it go, bothering it with a spray bottle, even as its leaves fluttered away.

One frigid December morning I tunneled into Manhattan on the A train. I'd read an essay by Oliver Sacks about the New York Fern Society and its monthly gatherings at the Bronx Botanical Garden. On the journey north, nodding into my fleece, I fantasized about a place where nice white people in pith helmets and many-pocketed khakis might help.

The office was filled with fluorescent light and octogenarians in khakis. Earlier that week, I had bleached my hair platinum blond. My scalp stung as heat seeped into my winter coat and climbed my face. I took the seat closest to the door and politely paid attention to a washed-out slideshow of ornamental ferns in concentric circles on immaculate Westchester turfgrass.

"Why are you here?" the Fern Society members gently asked, after the presentation. I told them that a plant I loved had died. When I told them I was there so that I could learn what a fern was, they told me about the other Oriental who usually came. She wasn't here today, they said, and I was relieved and horrified. I touched my scalp; it was on fire and flaking onto my sweater.

In a large glass bowl near the front of the room, a brown resurrection plant turned green as it became saturated with water, opening like a hand. A rock-faced man presented exquisitely detailed paintings of ferns, their fiddleheads and fronds carved into cross sections, not a single fine hair on a rhizome missed. There was a brief lecture about the specimen the society had discovered on a recent trip to China. When I asked questions, it was as if my voice were someone else's. I was too self-conscious to listen to their answers.

They were kind, but I never went back.

AT FIRST, THE FERNS WERE INSCRUTABLE. The differences between bracken and grass, maidenhair and ivy, were invisible. I couldn't tell one spray of green from another, didn't know there was a difference between a true fern and a fern ally. Instead, I was drawn in by their language.

Instead of leaves, for instance, ferns have *pinnules* (the tiniest petallike leaves) and *pinna* (a set of them, waving from the body of the fern like a feather). Instead of stems or stalks, there are *petioles*. You call the full articulation of *pinnae*, without the petiole, a *blade*. If you include the petiole, it becomes a *frond*. The brown wisps sweeping the floor beneath them are *rhizomes*.

The colloquial names of ferns can be matter-of-fact and unassuming, describing exactly how a specimen looks: ostrich ferns look like they belong on an ostrich. The leaves of filmy ferns, whose vascular tissue is only one cell wide, are as gossamer. In other instances, fern names are mystical: there are adder's-tongues, polypodies, cliff brakes, and club moss. Maidenhairs, quillworts, glassworts, spleenworts, and moonworts. Crystal orbs and dark, velveted rooms. The universe pouring into blank human eyes, the plane between consciousness and dreams and death.

The Victorians believed that to dream of ferns was a sign of magic, a blessing of courage and curiosity. But modern interpretations of ferns revealing themselves in one's unconscious are less optimistic. It's said that tracing the delicate fronds of a fern in a dream, winding through their fractal divisions, their obsessive symmetry, might indicate a deadening of pleasure: anxiety, a premonition of illness, restlessness, fear.

My dreams pulse with suggestions of my brother. His voice sweeps past me like a breeze. An unexpected hand on my shoulder. The familiar twitching of a mouth. A thickly woven sweater. Upon waking, I am filled with warmth like a heavy blanket. But then, the rapid, unwelcome splitting of self into what is past and what is present, what is real and what has sputtered from my longing unconscious. The images, the emotions dissipating fast, a silk tearing from my hand. The unwaking is a tunnel that descends into the earth indefinitely, though it lasts for one, two breaths. And as the present moment, lucid as daylight, invents itself around me, brilliant, thrilling, and vast, I ponder the buzzing dawn, and wonder if there is truth in anything new.

CHAPTER 2 \\\\

LITTLE SEED STARTED as an idea at once invisible and overt, jimmied together from insecurity, hope, longing, envy, thin air. She was the legend on a foreign map. She was a home made unfamiliar by darkness.

We are not like other Chinese people, Baba says when the lights come on. *You are not like other Chinese people*, Baba says to her, gentle but stern. What does that mean? she wonders briefly, before pleasure and security wash over her. Baba is a little heavyset, with salt-and-pepper hair. He wears a cotton T-shirt tucked into corduroy slacks, and his big head and square face are trustworthy and warm, in the way that the faces of philosophers and shar-peis are benevolent, their smiles snug in too much skin.

They are sitting in a study. It is dim, the only light the in-

7

candescence radiating from a lamp on a ponderous cherry desk, carved with peonies and whorls of ocean. The walls are lined with bookcases, the bookcases filled with tomes on religion, philosophy, art, and botany. The shelves exhibit a desire to know, to examine, and to become. One corner is busy with Chinese restaurant menus. Another sags under titles in English: *How to Dress Like a Gentleman*, *How to Raise a Lady*.

He waves his hand, and images of a city, green and boulevarded, shimmer before her. He tells her of a faraway place called Shanghai, a glamorous whirl of Eastern and Western cosmopolitanism. Ladies in diamonds and clingy qibaos sway to jazz. Men in waistcoats nurse martinis late into the night, trying out American slang. Baba is there, destined to be a scholar, he says, proudly handing her a yellowing manuscript of Chekhov's *The Seagull* that he translated into Chinese as a young man. But he was born too late—the imperial examination was abolished long before he came along.

He sighs. No matter. He was fortunate to be tutored by some of the greatest minds of Shanghai in Buddhism, English, feng shui, and poetry, among other subjects, because these men were the patients of his grandfather, a prominent Shanghai physician. He studied at their knees, poring over books in the town houses of the French Concession, under the immense shade of the plane trees of Weihai Lu, their white bark peeling from the trunks like newsprint. Nanxiang Lu, with its dumplings and ice-cold soy milk, lies just beyond the trees. Further still and the Bund unrolls along the tranquil Huangpu River, where Baba would stroll as the afternoon deepened. This is where he lived before America, with Little Seed's Mama and Big Brother and all of their ancestors, each of them not like other Chinese people and bestowing upon Little Seed the gift of being a different sort of Chinese person.

Baba returns to the beginning. *In China, we were like the Kennedys*, he says without a hint of irony, in the language of Shanghai. If speaking Shanghainese is already a signal of status, the fossilized Shanghainese of her family is even stranger: a pre-Revolution accent that has lain coiled in a single home in Tennessee now for a generation. *You know the Kennedys? Yes. But then the Communists confiscated and destroyed everything during the Cultural Revolution. Your mother couldn't go to college, your grandmother tore up her own wedding photos and flushed them down the toilet, your great-grandfather, the prominent doctor, ended his career sweeping the streets.* He omits an aunt, a painter, who killed herself by jumping out of a window. *Worse, all the knowledge of ancient Chinese and its history and culture burned. It's all gone now.* He shakes his head, then looks at Little Seed and smiles a little sadly before straightening up. *But now we are in America, and we are Americans. And, we have you.* He gathers up the images and books and files them away.

He still remembers that first night, when he picked Mama and Big Brother up from the airport in the United States. They had just arrived from Shanghai, where they lived apart from him for seven years while he made a home for them in America. He walked them out onto the overpass of the highway near their new home as dusk settled over the streets and lights of the buildings in the distance began to flicker on. Big Brother rested his arms and chin on the railing, marveling over the complexities of make, the sheer number of vehicles humming steadily along the two lanes of freeway. And as darkness fell, beams of red and white light passed across his face, and he asked Baba if everything in America was so beautiful.

From then on, Baba knew it was his responsibility to invent their world, fit together the pieces, without knowing if he would ever be right. But he started at the beginning and kept inventing words for the pieces of their life and their home. He is currently working on some future stuff too, but it's a tedious task that requires a lot of nimbleness in the present moment given complex factors in the time-space continuum—*you wouldn't understand, the Chinese is too complicated*—but Little Seed has nothing to worry about, she is part of this story too, even if he's still testing out some ways to write her in. One thing is certain: Baba will always take care of her, no matter what, that's his duty as a father. And Mama and Big Brother will support her in ways that those who are not blood never will. *We asked Big Brother if he wanted a sister, and he said he did, which is why we decided to have you. So to him you owe your life.* Little Seed can rely on them—that's what family is for. What comes next is up to her. Being a doctor, like Baba, would be good, or an attorney, of course. But what about a famous actress, or a columnist for *Newsweek*? The president, even. *Don't laugh; of course it can happen.*

For hours he regales her, then for days, then for years. She feels she can go on listening to him forever, if only he will keep filling the air. But pulsating in the back of her mind as he fills every inch of her with story is a question that pokes above the surface and sinks immediately. Here it is again, before it leaves: *What about me?*

DOWN WITH BIG BROTHER.

Baba's wail shatters Little Seed's pond-still reflection. She's stunned, watching him like an approaching train. His gaze is faraway. The air reverberates. Bits of dust drift down from the books. Where did Baba go? Was it his voice, or a voice contained within him? Was he sent into the past by her form, small enough to recall the Red Guards who once denounced him? Does he want to overthrow Big Brother, and if so, why?

Baba's face returns to the present a little, and she feels hesitant but optimistic. Come back to me, Baba.

EXECUTE LITTLE SEED.

As with many children of insane parents, a curious thing happens within her when Baba starts denouncing her, or other members of the family. She hears what Baba is saying and scrubs the words of their meaning as they arrive. They're no longer words but alarms that shut down her senses; her mind is an empty room. His eyes look past her, flashing at each word. She barely hears his voice now. She makes counterinventions. The carpet is moss. The bookshelves are trees. Baba is a windup monkey left in the forest.

The color eventually returns to Baba's face, the movement to his body. He lifts his forgotten cup of tea and takes a sip. Little Seed searches his face. Is he back? She still wants stories of a glittering and eternal Shanghai, of her banished aristocratic family.

He smiles a little bashfully. He looks away and inhales as if to begin a sentence, but darts back to his desk, as if he has remembered something that can't wait. He's swept away, snatching a pen, raiding a desk drawer, fingers flying, eyes wide.

LITTLE SEED THINKS TO ASK MAMA about the denouncements, what they really mean, as Mama brushes out Little Seed's hair while she sits on the bathroom counter. *Your hair has gotten so long,* she says, untangling a knot with a wide-tooth comb. *It's thick just like your Baba's but straight like mine,* she says, and Little Seed feels proud hearing the glow in Mama's voice, to feel that she is in possession of their collected goodness.

Does Baba really want Big Brother and me to die? Little Seed asks, calmed by the cool tip of the comb as Mama divides the hemispheres of her head. Mama pauses and pushes air through her teeth, still holding Little Seed's hair in both hands, and she knows she's done something wrong.

Don't listen to him, she whispers. An admonition. *Don't take it seriously*, she says. *Just let it go in one ear and out the other.* How? Little Seed wonders. *I've tried to get him to change; I try to yell at him*, Mama says now, a little gentler, and then, finally, resigned: *He just wants to yell that stuff all the time.* Mama ties back her hair into two tails, and when she's done, she sits down so her face is level with Little Seed. She lowers her voice.

You have to remember that Baba's childhood was very bitter, she says. *His baba and mama abandoned him as a child, and no one cared for him. When I met him in Shanghai, he didn't even have an extra change of clothing or a bed to sleep in. Then he was locked away in student prison by the Red Guards for months during the Cultural Revolution and sent to Xi'an for reeducation. He doesn't know what a good family is supposed to be like*, she says, tying red ribbons around Little Seed's ponytails. Basic vocabulary for this family: *Cultural Revolution, Communists, Red Guards, counterrevolutionaries, to reeducate, to denounce, to lock up.*

But your baba is a good baba, she says. *He works very hard and takes care of all of us. Look at this nice house, look at your beautiful pink dress.* Little Seed pats her shimmering taffeta skirt. She studies Mama's face, a smooth powdered oval nestled in shiny permed curls, her lips painted deep red. She takes Little Seed's hands in hers. *And anyway*, she says, *don't be scared. He'll always listen to me, because he's scared to lose me. Sometimes I think about him, and I feel that I'm not only his wife but also his mother, because he didn't have one. I feel sorry for him*, she says.

What are you talking about? Baba's voice enters the room

before his body does, and Mama stands up and straightens her body, shielding Little Seed's vision. *I was telling her about Shanghai and the Revolution*, she says. There is a long moment of silent combat that Little Seed feels between her parents, though she isn't party to their eyes.

Little Seed deserves to know about the past, about her family, Mama says sharply.

Enough, Baba says, before she finishes the sentence, raising his voice enough that she sees Mama's body stiffen. *Those stories end with me*, he says.

CHAPTER 3 \\\\ Spores

FERNS BEGIN WITH SPORES instead of seeds. A *spore* is a single-celled reproductive unit capable of generating life on its own, without sexual interaction. This is what distinguishes the fern from the nonfern. Trees, cacti, flowers, and vegetables require fruit and the lavish colors of flowers to attract birds, bats, and honeybees to reproduce—they are reliant on the community of other creatures to create a new generation. But ferns don't ascend into fervent color each spring, they don't rely on pollen to be carried from anther to pistil, they don't wrap a seed in fruit. Instead, they set golden dust into the wind, each microscopic speck a potential new fern borne over stretches of ocean and desert.

Reproducing by spores has meant that ferns are often the first species to repopulate razed areas, carried terrific distances by breezes, over land and sea. They make a home of catastrophe: hurricanes, forest fires, a fallen tree, their spores propagating easily on the freshly agitated soil. After the volcanic eruption of Mount St. Helens in 1980, for instance, the ashen, rocky outcrops were soon grown over by the tangled beginnings of ferns, their leaves unfurling like afternoon shadow—the spores of at least one species had crossed the Pacific Ocean from Japan.

Yet, unlike other spore-bearing creatures such as moss and fungi, ferns express their spores in visible clusters on the backs of their leaves, enclosures called *sporangia*. Sporangia cluster in precise, elaborate patterns called *sori*. Perfect buttons in columns of two or three, zigzagging lines, fat herringbones, chevrons, the most finely drawn crosshatch. Enormous bird's-nest ferns, whose leaves are like wide lengths of ribbon, exhibit fine lines of rust-colored spores so exact that I can't help but imagine someone doing the same slow work with a ruler and pencil down a sheet of paper. Some sori grow so enthusiastically that, when fertile, they appear like orange clumps of fish roe, heavy under the belly of a leaf. And on some bracken, sori form unbroken lines just within the edges of a leaf, tracing the backs like golden stitching.

Some sori are covered by a papery tissue called an *indusium*. Indusia are as elaborately diverse as sori and are often a key to the correct identification of a species: indusia can be *peltate* (round and attached to sori at the center, like a dimple), reniform (kidney-shaped), or cup-shaped, among other forms. Their purpose is to protect the sori, and once the sporangia are mature, the indusia shrivel to expose the mature spores.

When enlarged under a microscope, spores can be quite beautiful. The single cells, magnified to the size of a planet, come in two primary shapes—bean or onigiri—and a range of colors, from pale yellow to red to black. Magnified lycopodium spores look like half-moons of coral, their walls porous and fragile. The spores of bladder ferns look like they're covered in Astroturf. The ribbon fern's spores look like salted plums.

UNTIL THE INVENTION OF THE MICROSCOPE, the reproductive cycle of ferns was hidden from observation, which stoked wild speculation about magic, that fern seeds were of another realm. While flowers and trees produced observable fruit and seeds, ferns had gold dust on the backs of their leaves. Preindustrial Western cultures spun fables about the lengths one had to go to collect fern seed, and the glories one might experience upon doing so.

One German fable tells of a hunter who shot at the sun overhead on Midsummer Day. Drops of blood dripped from the sky. Collected into a handkerchief, the blood quickly dried into fern seed. The seeds allowed the hunter to harness powers of the occult, to find gold or other treasures.

Another story from Germany instructs fern-seed collectors to forgo church, prayers, and holy water in the weeks leading up to Christmas. Then, between the hours of eleven o'clock and midnight on Christmas Eve, at the crossing of two roads where bodies have been carried on their way to burial, a procession of their beloved dead arrive. The fern collector must remain silent or die. Eventually, the devil passes, the last figure in the ghostly procession, and delivers the fern seed. Worn on the body, the seed grants the strength of thirty men, wealth, and power.

In keeping with the German stories, Victorian fern enthusiasts believed that placing fern seeds in one's pocket called forth a veil of invisibility. The process, by then, had become easier than withstanding the devil's unsparing trials. One simply had to carry twelve pewter plates into the forest and stack them under the leaves of bracken on the eve of Midsummer Day. At midnight, it was said, the fern would briefly exhibit blue flowers from which its seed would tumble, slipping through the metal of eleven plates before collecting on the twelfth.

But why would anyone ever want to be invisible, I thought, as I learned of each of these fables. What is the fascination? I would rather be rich, I would rather be blond and tall and unquestionably beautiful, I would rather have breasts and an ass that everyone admires. I would rather empty my head of all that agonizes me. I would rather remain ignorant of the shifting stories my parents tell, of the pain that sometimes lies dormant and sometimes erupts in my father. To desire invisibility is to know already what it is like to be seen, to see your disappearance as a lark, rather than as inevitability or as necessity.

I think of how ferns, so starkly different in their anatomy and reproduction and phylogeny, are indistinguishable from other plants, their differences invisible to unobservant eyes. Invisibility isn't the only form of disappearance, I think. You might also just learn the correct rituals, the right things to say, lie about your discomfort, omit the details just enough to come a little closer to what surrounds you.

I already disappear, I think to myself. I can't help but disappear. I read the only texts I can find or that I'm given. They tell stories of people who don't look like me, who aren't my ancestors, in a language that is foreign to my family and native to me. And so I am erased, first from the page, then from the room in which I am reading, and then from the world around me. I am nowhere, I am nothing, without needing to capture fern seed, without trying.

CHAPTER 4 \\\\

THE SOUND OF LITTLE SEED'S HOME is either on or off. When it is on, Mama and Baba's arguments ring through Little Seed's home, their shrieking so metallic she can't make out the words, even at close range. When she asks about the arguments, she is told that this is just how Chinese people are. This is Chinese culture. Anything can set off their noise, but lately, Big Brother's difficulties in school are the catalyst.

His English is still lumbering. Why didn't they enroll him in language classes when he first came? And his slow comprehension means he is falling behind in all of his classes, even math, which was his refuge when he first arrived eight years ago. Arabic numerals translate. And he spends most of his days looking after Little Seed—teaching her to whistle and snap, making her ice cream sundaes, showing her how to swim and ride a bike. She loves to sit with him in front of the television screen on the blue carpet as he watches meticulously taped episodes of *Star Trek* all afternoon, mouthing the English words back to the screen. Soon, it will be time to apply to colleges, and neither Baba nor Mama confronts that his slow assimilation may imperil his future as a physician. In this home, there is no other path for Big Brother. It must be his own fault. So Baba calls him lazy and stupid, and Mama tries to protect him, and the sound begins again, like thunder.

When the sound is turned off, it is because Mama has become so frustrated during these arguments that she walks out the front door and pretends to leave entirely. Where could Mama possibly go, outside of this house, when she barely speaks English, barely drives?

Or the sound turns off because Baba has decided to give Big Brother the silent treatment to punish him, smiling sweetly at Little Seed as Big Brother, on the verge of tears, attempts to win his attention by asking if Baba would like some water or some Sprite. *Baba, Baba, Baba*, he begs, in a child's tone, though he is old enough now to be mistaken for Little Seed's father as he rides her around the neighborhood on his shoulders. Little Seed learns that Baba can erase Big Brother from his vision for weeks. Is this *Chinese* behavior? Is this what it means to be *Chinese*?

There is an expectation, however, that as quiet or as loud as the house becomes during the day, all four of them assemble politely for dinner, which Mama prepares each afternoon according to Baba's exacting standards. She was a musician in Shanghai and hated domestic work, but in America she feels it is her duty. *Baba speaks English well, so he goes into the world and makes money, so the least I can do is work hard inside the house to make sure everyone is healthy.*

Every family member is assigned a different color plate,

which Baba has calculated according to the ancient practice of *bagua*. (Again, the Chinese is too complicated for you to understand.) Mama's plates are blue, Baba's plates are red, Little Seed's are green, and Big Brother's are yellow, and the colors all correspond to a desire for future success. The family members sit at the round table quietly like the four points of a compass. Little Seed eases into her seat knowing that they are constrained by the rhythm of food served and eaten.

Mama sets a small dish of braised cucumbers by her plate, dyed black and auburn with soy, and gives Little Seed the serving spoon. Little Seed is at the age where she is picky about what she will and will not eat, but she reliably likes the slightly sweet and savory vegetable. As she scoops a pile into her rice bowl, she hears Baba whimper from across the table, and she removes her hands as quickly as possible.

Why does she get special treatment?, he says quietly, and Little Seed begins her retreat within, frantically attempting to recall Mama's advice about letting words pass into one ear and out the other. She tries to find a place inside of her to go, to become invisible. But then there is the loud thud on the table, the reverberations rattling the plates and her forearms on the table, and Little Seed sees that Baba has clenched his right hand in a fist and his searching eyes are lit with anger. She uses her imagination to dull the sound, dull the shake.

Then Mama is saying, in an absurdly calm voice, that Baba is crazy and that she wishes she had never married him. Baba is screaming that she only cares about Big Brother and Little Seed. The light leaves Big Brother's face, and he carefully folds up his napkin, perches his chopsticks on his plate, stands up, and slams his chair into the table before walking away. Little Seed is determined to follow him, to slam her chair out of anger and indignation too, and begins folding her napkin.

Little Seed, stay, Mama instructs, piling food onto her plate, and Little Seed is frozen. She sits with her head bowed so she cannot see Mama's or Baba's face as she finishes her food. *He's a good baba*, she thinks. *Look at these beautiful plates with their rich varnish, look at this beautiful pink shirt Little Seed gets to wear.*

LATER THAT NIGHT, the sound in the house is on, and Big Brother finds Little Seed playing in her room alone. He pulls her by the hand down the hallway, away from where Mama's and Baba's shadows cut into each other in the lemon light of the kitchen as they argue. He looks back at her, an enormous silver bag of potato chips in his hand, and smiles reassuringly as he leads her out the side door, into the grass, onto the gray cement driveway.

She knows that something good lies ahead, if they can just get there. They climb into his car, and for a moment she worries that Mama and Baba will hear them leaving, so late. The wordless, metallic ringing of their voices still feels hot on her brain when she closes her eyes.

Are you ready? Big Brother asks, and she locates her bravery and tells him that she is, though she feels her smile quivering. He turns the engine on and places his right arm behind her headrest as he turns to back out, and she studies his handsome freckled face, the blue-gray print of his sideburns, his thick black hair swept to one side. His jaw is tense, but there is quiet in his eyes. The night sky blooms around them as they descend from the driveway into the street, and she smiles at the pure expanse, at the feeling of leaving.

They tear through the neighborhood, lampposts ticking by, the stars fixed in the black sky as they pass the dark houses of their neighbors, horses at pasture, heads low and ponderous in dark grass, the low-slung strip malls pulsing firefly yellow from fluorescent lights. She sees it all as if it's her first experience of freedom and safety.

Do you know the girls at school? Little Seed asks as they merge onto the freeway, the pendant moon hanging before them.

Which ones? Big Brother glances at her, eyebrows furrowed.

The ones who are mean to me, she says, certain she'd told him before.

How are they mean to you? he asks. She shrugs, not wanting to disrupt the peaceful expanse of black unrolling before them, the way he whips between the lines on the freeway, talk radio humming low.

They say they don't like me because I'm different, she says. He hits the gas a little, and she jolts forward. She turns from the moon to look at him. His eyes are narrowed and his jaw is clenched. The air whipping past them cools a few degrees.

You are different, he says, eyes on the road. *You're better than them.*

She wants to protest: How can he even know? What if they are right? But she's flooded by his reassurance. An intoxicating warmth radiates from her solar plexus through her face, into her fingertips. And as she turns, limb by limb, into pure light, she observes that the universe within this small car—its cheap gray upholstery, its chemical smell, far from their parents, far from school—is entirely still. The outside world whips past, shape-shifts in its motion, in its unpredictability, yet in this ten cubic feet of plastic and rubber, there is peace.

Big Brother reaches forth, taps the radio with his index finger, and fills the new quiet by humming a melody, just one note following another. It's a chorus to a Chinese lullaby that Little Seed begs to hear played each night on the tape recorder before she falls asleep. The words are written from the perspective of a brother comforting his younger sister as he prepares to leave home for war.

The clouds in the sky worry. The grass on the ground worries too.

Little Seed looks at Big Brother, and he smiles briefly as he continues humming. Little Seed closes her eyes, and the sound of his voice is warm and familiar against the sound of wind whipping past the car.

Worry cannot keep the clouds from separating.

And worry cannot keep the grass from being cut low.

Her body melts into a dense and invisible thing as she follows his wordless voice within the last light of her mind, until it is the only faint thing from outside of herself that she can recognize.

Dear sister, please let go of my hand. It's okay; I am ready to go.

IT'S LATE WHEN THEY RETURN HOME, and Little Seed tiptoes back to her room while Big Brother cleans up the car. On the way, she notices a line of dragon figurines in the hall, positioned in an arc, as if to attack the door to Big Brother's bedroom. They are mostly her toys, given to her by relatives, because she is an Earth Dragon in the Chinese zodiac.

The one in the middle is her favorite, painted reflective gold and clutching an iridescent glass sphere in its mouth. She already knows what has happened, who has placed her toys there, and why. But she wills her brain to skip over this part of the narrative, as well as the part where the toys must have been searched for and stolen from the piles in her room. She gathers up her dragons in her arms and wearily pulls them into bed with her.

I HAVE SOMETHING WE CAN DO, Mama says mischievously one afternoon, her eyes sparkling. Baba is napping, Big Brother is with friends, and Little Seed is bored.

Do you hear Baba snoring? Mama says. Little Seed nods. It's unpleasant, like construction outside a window when she's playing house with her stuffed animals. Like Monkey setting a theater fire. Mama reaches next to the bed and produces a silver tape deck. Little Seed is perplexed, but Mama touches her index finger to her lips and motions for Little Seed to follow her across the hall.

She places the tape deck down in front of her and Baba's bedroom and clicks the record button. The small red circle flutters on, and Little Seed is wide-eyed, clapping her hand over her mouth so she doesn't laugh and wake Baba up.

Mama cuts the deck, and they tiptoe back to Little Seed's room. On the bed, they play the tape of Baba's snores, which are distorted to sound like fierce wind or breaking waves on a shoreline.

It sounds like a monster, Little Seed says, laughing so hard, her head hurts.

It sounds like a tiger roaring, Mama says, her voice pitched high, like a delighted child.

They play it back over and over the rest of the afternoon, laughing so hard they roll on their backs on the bed until they are gasping for air and wiping their eyes. In Little Seed's mind, for a moment, Baba is just a tiny animal locked in a silver machine.

SUMMER IS FADING AND it's decided that Big Brother will continue to live at home while he attends the university in town, where Baba works. Mama and Baba collaborate for days over his course schedule, plotting the route to his best future. The house is quiet with something that feels like pride, or at least anticipation. Little Seed watches as Baba ties a handsome watch around Big Brother's wrist, and Big Brother wipes tears from his eyes as he touches its face.

Little Seed knows nothing of the future, but she comes to learn or understand that life begins when you leave home. She thinks of Big Brother driving away, she remembers the horses at pasture, the beautiful blue light of the moon, and she imagines what form he might take, what color, when he is allowed to adventure.

The family goes to buy supplies that Big Brother will need when he begins his classes. As they are checking out, Little Seed pulls Big Brother by his hand as hard as she can, wanting badly to run out onto the asphalt of the parking lot with him, and play tag or be spun around in an enormous circle.

Mama has already told her that once Big Brother leaves for school, she'll have to be a big girl and care for herself, so she is trying her best to borrow his attention now, before it runs out. Big Brother doesn't budge as she pulls on him. Her rubber sneakers squeak against the tile as she laughs and calls his name again and again.

CHAPTER 5 \\\ Prothallium

ON SUITABLE GROUND, where there is water and sunlight, fern spores press themselves into a tiny heart-shaped green growth several millimeters long called a *prothallium*, on the fallen trunks of trees, or in the wet forest underbrush. This isn't a fern, exactly. It's just another beginning, a gametophyte form that is free-living, comprising all necessary structures for reproduction. (The gametophytes of *angiosperms*, seed-bearing plants, exist separately as male or female counterparts in pollen or in flowers, and require animals or insects to transfer one to the other for successful mating.)

Instead, a *zygote* forms on the underside of the heart-shaped prothallium leaf, and the prothallium, in turn, nurtures this new, delicate embryo through photosynthesis until the embryo grows into a small plant capable of turning sun into food and drawing water up through hairlike roots on its own. Eventually, the prothallium falls away (a sacrifice), and what is left is what will grow taller and taller into the plant we call fern.

Not all prothallia grow ferns, however. Some have evolved, instead, to exist in their interstitial gametophyte form. The rare weft fern, *Trichomanes intricatum*, which is common in the Northeast and throughout the Appalachian mountain range, where I grew up, looks more like moss or algae, blooming like a jade cloud over the walls of darkened caverns and their perennially wet overhangs. Up close, *Trichomanes* appears like so many tangled emerald threads, spangled by flashes of dew.

On their tips, the weft fern has evolved to produce *gemmae*, tiny asexual buds, which drop and produce more gametophytes, forgoing entirely the development of fronds and spores. Instead, they exist in interstices, not quite seed, not quite fern. They turn noncalcareous rock into emerald carpets, with this mossy tendency.

Somewhere along the way, scientists hypothesize, it was just more advantageous for *Trichomanes* to evolve for hidden places, low to the ground, easily mistaken for moss. Practically invisible, flourishing in nowheres, dependent only on itself for reproduction and survival.

AS I WANDERED THROUGH ALL THESE STARTS, I encountered others who had turned to ferns when they were lost. There was once a British naturalist named Edward Newman in Victorian England who was prescribed three months of a walking cure after falling into a depression. At that time, walking in nature was a common prescription for ailments, both physical and emotional. Newman was the youngest son of a Quaker family, expected to take on his father's business of ropemaking, but his heart lay in natural history, the fine observation of small creatures and all that was green. He filled his spare time writing and editing journals dedicated to plants, animals, and insects, even as he obediently dedicated himself to ropemaking.

When he finally accepted an offer for the family business to be acquired, he became totally depressed, overcome by the certainty of his own failure and the terrifying release from what came before, a history that contained certainty, his family, a clear path. Newman, on the advice of a doctor, set out to tour Wales, moving slowly through windy mountains kept damp by the blowing Irish Sea. He became fixated on the ferns he saw as he walked, endeavoring to capture each variety, learn their names, and sketch their individual natures.

His explorations were bound into a small volume called *A History of British Ferns and Allied Plants* and published, to enormous acclaim, in 1840. The book sold out again and again as Victorians throughout Britain turned its neatly cataloged pages and felt for themselves the delirious urgency of going into the world to locate maidenhair, spleenwort, and bracken. The ensuing fifty-year period was called *Pteridomania*, or fern fever. Women in crinolines and parasols crowded forests and dales in search of ferns. Extravagant prices were paid for rare specimens. Many varieties nearly became extinct from overharvesting. It became all the rage to cultivate gardens so exact that it was as if the ferny wilderness had appeared whole outside one's window.

What happened to Newman? It was his story to begin with—easy to forget that all this fern madness began as a quieter form of illness, agony turned outward, made direct. Did he find what he was looking for? Or did he get buried, like his story, by the churning of the outside world?

All I know is that after ferns, he got into ghosts: Newman

founded a journal in 1843 called *Zoologist*, whose aim was to make natural history accessible to nonexperts, "to combine scientific truths with readable English." The publication opened its pages to reader submissions and published the observations of well-known naturalists alongside laypeople.

In 1847, Newman started publishing reports of sea serpent sightings. At the time, entertaining the idea that the cryptid might be real was eccentric, to say the least. (Imagine if *National Geographic* ran regular bigfoot sightings.) But Newman believed that there had to be truth behind the reports of sea serpents: something in the natural world animated the stories; they couldn't all be hoaxes. It's easy to dismiss ghost stories if you're fixated on measurement, but their underpinnings are as real as any story. The water, the glimmer of movement, the shadow of something fantastic. To Newman, that was worth ink. Later, he published sightings of moa and woolly mammoth.

I MIGHT HAVE HAD an easier time stepping into the world of ferns had present-day Tennessee or New York been steeped in fern madness. It would have been nice to adjust to my external circumstances, rather than obsessively pulling out threads from books and scattered internet archives.

At the height of the Victorian fern craze, Pteridomania, blades of ferns were carved into the stone capitals of building columns, set into the faces of tables, dressers, and cabinets as glimmering inlays. Lace makers spun their fronds into delicately woven white squares, precise to species-specific spore patterns on the back of each pinnule. The fascination flowed outward from the home too, and with the modern ease of train travel, Victorians spilled into the countryside to search for new ferns to admire, digging them up to bring home to perfectly cultivated gardens.

Those who lived in the countryside could make a fortune gathering local specimens and selling them to visitors at the train station. For a premium, tourists might even persuade locals to guide them to dig the ferns themselves, or at least observe them in their natural habitat. But often, the scouts would demur by saying that the localities were simply too treacherous.

Often, they were. Injuries and deaths were common in the years of fern fever, given that ferns often make their homes in the shadows—in the crevices of escarpments, in dolomite outcrops, on waterfall brinks, scrambling on tree bark. Fern enthusiasts occasionally disappeared without notice to seek a rare specimen, and at least one was found dead.

It was dangerous too for the ferns most admired. Countless British varieties nearly went extinct during this era of obsession, and as attention to ferns expanded across seas—to Ireland and Wales, then eventually the United States—precious fern ecosystems were also endangered, roots pulled indiscriminately from the earth. I feel a particular grief from the desolation of groves of the Australian tree ferns, which were destroyed by tourism and poaching.

To imagine tree ferns is to slip into something like deep time, to see the present moment held fast by threads of what came before. In my mind, I picture a deceptively slender trunk, made sturdy by rhizomes winding themselves into a tightly tangled wool around a tender stem, so impenetrable that chain saws have been known to seize when taken to one. Split open into a cross section, the trunk's soft center looks like a starburst, and the wavy rhizomes surrounding it resemble the folds of a brain. This sturdy architecture supports the tree fern to climb high—nearly one hundred feet tall in some species. At the very top grows a crown of furry ocher croisers, each as thick as a wrist. They unravel into a parasol of enormous, finely toothed fronds, each as tall as a person and as wide as their wingspan. Walking beneath them, one sees day-light stitched into delicate, ever-shifting filigree.

Tree ferns are rare today, despite growing conservation efforts, and when I think of them, I can think only of endings. Their present, rapid extinction. And, remarkably, how little they have changed in nearly three hundred million years of history, one of the only species that remain of the flora that was buried deep underground millions of years ago during the Carboniferous period and transformed since by heat and pressure into coal. I've read that if you crack open pieces of coal, you might find fern traces inside.

NEAR THE END OF FERN MADNESS, enthusiasts learned that by staying put, one might avoid harming or being harmed by the ferns and their environment. Newman had a close friend named Nathaniel Bagshaw Ward, who began successfully bringing ferns into the home by cultivating them in glass cases sealed onto wooden bases. The structures, known as Wardian cases, retained moisture and heat while protecting the ferns from the pervasive smoke from a society now powered by coal.

Within Wardian cases, fantasies could be cultivated and kept safe. The early terrariums came in an extravagance of shapes, evoking birdcages, gazebos, temples, and towers. Among humidity-loving filmy ferns and maidenhairs, the Victorians displayed their collections of minerals and coral. They constructed replicas of ruins and follies set into sloping hills of sandstone and moss. Condensation collected on the slopes of the glass, surreally misting the tiny worlds within. Romance was key: The focus of one of Ward's own cases was a tiny replica of the west window of Tintern Abbey, fashioned out of pumice and stone.

But imaginations spilled underneath even the largest Wardian cases, and eventually, Victorians began glazing shut the bay windows of their homes and filling the space between the panes with ferns, lycopods, mosses, then seawater, aquatic plants, beetles, and fish. Some windows comprised nearly self-regulating ecosystems that required little maintenance, just a balance of the right collection of beings. I love thinking about everything that must have gone into creating such a precise universe, the steady patience and observation required to be present to its workings, to fill it up and to pare it back, to worry over its individual course, all while existing apart from it. Is observation enough? Can such a world ever be real?

Cultivating such a window was also useful for reinventing whatever predictable, less beautiful views lay beyond one's parlor windows. Instead of the dreary gloom of shortening days and darkness, strangers lingering on the sidewalk, a picnic of gray, the dun dull city, one could gaze out on a crown of exotic fern fronds bending sweetly over a lush floor of club moss. Nearby, pumice stone stained velvet black from water rippling over it as small red fish darted back and forth below.

CHAPTER 6 \\\\

AFTER SWIM PRACTICE ONE AFTERNOON, Mama drags Little Seed from the locker room by the arm and toward the coach. Mama is frantic with broken English, and she points accusingly at a white boy whose face is raw with acne, still slick after emerging from the pool, and tugs away Little Seed's towel to reveal eczema rashes on the back of each of her thighs, scratched raw and bloody. The coach's eyes narrow, and she shakes her head, her voice patronizing and exasperated while she talks to Mama, as if she is coaxing a toddler out of a tantrum. The boy is concerned, hesitant. He observes their exchange, his fingers grazing the diving block.

The coach explains that the acne on his face is not contagious, could never have been passed through the chlorinated water to Little Seed, but Mama continues to yell, incomprehensible and furious. Little Seed is mortified, both at how the coach perceives Mama, as if she is a wild animal or an idiot; and at how Mama has brought the sound of their home into the outside world, has exposed her friends to it, in this place that she thinks of as her own. The patches of eczema sting as the chlorinated water evaporates, and she wants to scratch herself, or at least to cover the raw wounds with her hands so that no one can see.

Finally Mama yanks Little Seed's arm again and storms out of the gymnasium after telling the coach that Little Seed won't be returning. They drive home in silence, but later, Mama regales the family with the story at the dinner table as if it were a triumph. *That woman thought I was too stupid to figure it out*, Mama says, *but I made her regret ever discounting me. You should have seen her face!*

It was racism, Big Brother says quietly, leaning in and glancing at Baba tentatively. Baba smiles at him, and Big Brother relaxes. *She only treated you like that because you're not white.*

They look down on us because we're Chinese! Baba says. *How dare they think they can treat my wife like that. This is America. We are just as American as everyone else. What a useless idiot that woman is, what a turtle egg.* Little Seed's face turns red from embarrassment at hearing this insult, one of the very worst things a Shanghainese person might say about someone else: like the spores of ferns, turtle eggs are also unparented. Baba's face is now red with emotion and he is grinning from ear to ear and Big Brother is brighter as well, joined in protecting Mama and, by extension, Little Seed. Their words comfort Mama, who is now sitting back in her chair.

I'll drive a tank to her house and run her over! Baba says, and Little Seed can't help but laugh at the absurdity of what he says, imagining Baba in a tank, driving down the residential streets of her town. She has stopped observing violence in her weather. Baba and Mama are laughing too, and Baba's eyes grow soft.

Your Mama's English is so high quality. It's far better than mine, even, Baba says, with admiration that Little Seed senses is mocking. Mama's English isn't good, but she's also still learning. How is she supposed to get better when all of her time is spent in the home or raising Little Seed? But Mama preens in his attention and becomes bashful. *No one's English can compare to hers. It's so sophisticated and beautiful,* he continues.

That's enough, she says. *You always say that people become better at speaking a new language when they're really angry. That's all that happened.* And she goes back to passing around each of the four dishes she spent all afternoon preparing for dinner: red braised pork knuckles, bok choy glistening with garlic oil, peas with pork mince, and tiny freshwater shrimp, steamed in salted water.

A FRIEND FROM THE POOL calls Little Seed's house to ask if Little Seed can spend the night, and Little Seed feels glad that the connection to her life outside the home isn't broken. Her friend instructs her to put Mama on the line to speak with her own mother.

Mama speaks patiently into the phone in English, with great focus, nodding furiously and agreeing in a line of okays and offering dates and asking questions about where the friend's family lives, how Little Seed knows her. Little Seed listens impatiently, wanting to insert herself into the conversation and correct Mama's English, which Little Seed is fluent in, but she knows that others are not accustomed to Mama's mosaic English. Only she and Little Seed are fluent in this English, and Little Seed feels embarrassed and protective of its sudden, lush intimacy.

If they are at the grocery store or buying clothes at the mall, Little Seed often jumps in with her own English to translate what Mama is saying to the clerks when they appear confused at Mama's language, as much to help Mama as to protect her from the unkind glares and small-town closed-mindedness. But on the other side of a landline, Little Seed is unable to do anything but wait and listen to every syllable Mama makes and guess at what the voice on the other end of the line makes of her.

Finally, Mama writes a date down on a piece of paper, and Little Seed snatches the phone back, relieved to be in control again and thrilled to dream with her friend about what they'll do during their time together. But her friend's mother is still on the line as Little Seed presses the cool plastic to her ear.

"Here, take it," the unfamiliar voice says, a little distant from the receiver. Then, angrily, "I can't fucking understand anything she says." Little Seed's entire body ignites hearing this as she cradles the phone to her ear and stills her posture so Mama won't know there's something wrong. (How dare she treat Mama like that! What a useless idiot!) Mama has wandered away to another task and smiles at her. Little Seed intuits how challenging even a small exchange in English can be for Mama and feels they should both be proud at the ease with which she accomplished something so mundane but also so important. How many people in Tennessee have ever even tried to speak a new language? Little Seed forces herself to smile back at Mama as she waits for her friend to return to the phone.

BIG BROTHER FAILS OUT OF COLLEGE in a semester. Mama and Baba vacillate between blaming themselves for not preparing him and blaming him for his laziness and his inability to make a way out of their home. How will he succeed? How will he become the man he needs to be in order to carry on the family name, with his own wife, his own children, his own vocation? Mama and Baba worry that his inability to adjust to the outside world signals some greater moral or biological flaw. The noise in the house gets worse day by day as Mama and Baba fail to understand how Big Brother will rebuild the bridge to his destiny as a doctor. There's no other option for him except to emulate Baba's success.

Mama and Baba decide that Big Brother will enlist in the Navy, and soon he is packing his bags for boot camp in Chicago. Little Seed, who is seven, only knows the color, deep blue like the ocean at night, and she ponders the depths of what lies ahead. Mama and Baba hope the Navy will teach Big Brother discipline and order and transform him into the kind of person who seems, as Mama often says, like a *real man*. Every moment is to be occupied by the future.

Without someone to watch Little Seed lately, she is left to her own devices, architecting the first solar-powered city from her collection of stuffed animals, or authoring a biography of her future pet rabbit in crayon and iridescent tape. In her room, she is inclined toward mess; she likes to spend the day in all of her stuff—pretty crab shells foraged from the dinner table, enormous board books filled with drawings of animals. Relatives have started sending gifts that teach femininity—books come attached with ribbons to weave into her hair, enormous plastic rings and beads to make into necklaces. Little Seed has been attempting to paint her nails, but she lacks the motor skills to put on a coat evenly, so the ends of her fingers are forever tacky in lavender and robin's-egg blue.

Eventually Mama notices what looks to her like disarray. The comforter pulled over chairs flanked by Technicolor plush. There are stickers collaged onto furniture and candy wrappers in oyster piles. She loses her temper before Little Seed has even noticed her enter the room. And while Little Seed feels dismayed and a little afraid, she isn't particularly surprised to see that the noise has crept over the threshold of her room.

Little Seed withstands Mama's yelling about her mess and how little girls should be neat and orderly, but then Big Brother arrives at the door, and she trusts that Mama will immediately become self-conscious and stop freaking out. He'll defend her, like he always does. (He was the one who wanted her, so she owes him her life.)

Mama is quiet, and Big Brother walks over to her. Little Seed wants to smile, knowing that he'll be generous to her and Mama will feel sorry for being so mean. *I don't understand why my room can't be exactly how I want it*, Little Seed says quietly, emboldened by Big Brother's presence. But Big Brother frowns, his posture stiffens, and Little Seed knows she has miscalculated everything.

Don't you dare speak to Mama like that, he says. "You will respect me," he adds, now in English. And Little Seed feels terrified of this new, uncharted language between them, as if something unpleasant from the outside has been dragged in. She knows English only as authority, as something that knows far more than she does. It turns the space between them electric. "You will clean your room," he yells now, emphasizing every word as if each is a cliff off of which he is jumping. Little Seed looks to Mama, desperately hoping she can understand the nuance of his tone in English, the sterileness he is using at her, the distance, how wrong it all feels. The new voice Big Brother has found is powerful and menacing. Instead, Mama looks pleased. Here is a son who has found his masculine authority.

Little Seed closes her eyes and covers her face with her hands, frightened that more English will come. She feels him looming over her.

"At college, no one wants to date a girl whose nails are

chipped and ugly like that," he says. Little Seed tries to hide her nails by digging them deeper into her face, but she is too afraid to remove them entirely from her eyes. "You're never going to have a boyfriend," he says. "No one is ever going to want you."

ON A RARE OCCASION, Baba picks Little Seed up from school, and Little Seed feels nervous but excited to spend even a short time alone with him. She fantasizes: Baba asking her about her day, listening to her dreams and fears, listening to her moon over a boy she has a crush on. Baba lets Little Seed pick the radio station and appraises each pop song that blares on the radio approvingly, telling her about his life before Mama and Big Brother came to the States. When he was alone, he liked listening to the Bee Gees and the Beach Boys.

You're so smart and brave, Little Seed, and you have great taste, he says. *Your brother is smart too*, he continues, *but he's lazy. And you're smarter than him, anyway.* Little Seed wonders if it's true, and she feels the story he and Mama tell about Big Brother being worthless for failing out of school begin to crystallize.

Baba weaves expertly in and out of traffic, and continues chatting at her with a rare softness in his voice, and Little Seed feels conspiratorial in his attention. She would never be so lazy in school that she got bad grades and went to boot camp. She would work very hard, she would easily accomplish everything Mama and Baba set out for her. Or maybe she wouldn't need to even work that hard at it, if what Baba said was true, that she was naturally smarter than Big Brother. In any case, she'd never disappoint them like Big Brother has.

Little Seed, Baba says, making a turn, *do you know that I have a scar on my belly from when I was pregnant with you?* Little Seed tells him that no, she was in Mama's belly, not his.

No, Little Seed, I know Mama tells you that, but we had the doctor put you in my belly, and that is where you come from. Little Seed looks at him, and he is smiling, and suddenly she feels as though the space that is normally between them has vanished, that they are just playmates inventing a story together. One in which Little Seed is wanted. So badly wanted!

I don't believe you, Little Seed says, kicking her legs in front of her, and learning to play along.

Little Seed, you came from Baba's belly, he says, continuing the story. *So when will you let me cook you and eat you?* Little Seed screams in mock fear.

Will you let me eat you next year? Baba asks.

No, Little Seed says.

What about the year after that? he says.

No! Not then either, Little Seed says.

You have to say when you're going to let me eat you, Little Seed, Baba says, feigning disapproval. They pull into the garage, and Baba cuts the engine, crosses his arms, and looks to her, his face somber and waiting.

Little Seed looks back and feels the impossibility of continuing her father's story, feels her own ignorance of time. His eyes are earnest and patient as he waits for her answer, and she knows only that she would like to stay in this story for as long as she can, even if the terms are unsettling. Here, she is adored.

Okay, Baba, you can eat me in ten years, Little Seed says quietly, intimidated by the sound of the contract, but unable to think of a way out.

Ten years? Baba exclaims, clapping his hands on his face. *Little Seed, you haven't even been alive for ten years!* he says, and they both laugh so hard they weep and wipe their faces with their hands.

CHAPTER 7 \\\\ Fern

THE SLENDER STALK OF A NEW FERN, just shorn of its prothallium, resolves at its tip into a tightly clenched spiral called
a *fiddlehead* or a *crosier*, which recalls the apex of a snail's shell.
Croziers can be bare, a smooth green coil, or they can appear
scaly and matted, shrouded in a brown or white fur, the beginnings of fronds poking through their winding. A fiddlehead's
bind resembles a clenched fist or the way a snake looks, retreat-
ing after swallowing a rat. Over the course of days and weeks,
the crosier loosens its grip, straightening out into a rib studded
on both sides by leaves called *pinnae*, Latin for "wings."

Sometimes, petallike leaves splay out along the rib, like the
holly fern, which grows glossy emerald pinnae shaped like
cabochons. Other times ferns are fractal, and the pinnae are

croziers, too, that unravel just a beat behind the larger crosier. Those leaves might be divided into even smaller leaves; worlds unravel into worlds.

Given this fractal tendency, the structural nomenclature of their leaves relies on identifying divisions and subdivisions rather than committing to memory the exact shape or color of individual structures—what does it mean, in the end, to describe a leaf of a fern, when any one leaf may fork into many others? Instead, we describe ferns by the generations of their branching.

If the fiddlehead unravels into a single, undivided leaf, as in the case of a bird's-nest fern, with its leaves like long, wavy tape, we say that the fern is *simple* or *undivided*. If the fiddlehead unravels into a series of discrete pinnae, like the holly fern, or like the pearl-like cascade of maidenhairs, the ferns are *once-divided*. If once-divided leaves are discrete from the midrib, the fern is called *pinnate*. But if the leaves are fused to the midrib, like the upright combs of the common polypod, or of Boston ferns hanging from baskets on porches in summertime, they are called *pinnatifid*.

If a fiddlehead unravels into yet another series of fiddleheads that unravel into smaller leaves, called *pinnules*, these ferns are *twice-divided*—think of common ferns in forests, ostrich ferns and bracken, with their enormous triangular leaves, each pinnae pinched into rows of teeth. Rarer are the *thrice-divided* ferns, whose pinnules segment even further into impossibly tiny grooved teeth, called *ultimate segments*. They are ethereal, impossibly delicate, identified more by feeling than observation. The morning light in a lady fern or a hay-scented fern glows from within the lace of their fine architecture, as if woven in.

THE MECHANISM OF THE CROSIER—ITS tight grip as well as its spiraling—is called *circinate vernation*. Scientists say that the fern has developed the phenomenon in order to protect its *growing point* or its *apical meristem*, the tips of the leaves that contain cells capable of division and growth. The most tender part of the plant—the apex—is tucked in its deepest part, its most impenetrable core, as the rest of what will become what we think of as *fern* wraps around it snugly, in psychedelic strata. All of this formation for security, to preserve the next stage of growth, and eventually, the next generation.

My brain loses it a little identifying all the pathways back to the center, slips into a manic place attempting to find a fern structure that doesn't call back to the start: the tip of the frond is also the center of the spiral; the shape of the spiral leads back to where it started; all the little leaves tuck in, gesturing back to the origin point.

I try to cast out further in time—to the spores, to the sporangia, to the sori, to the prothalliums—but they all represent the fern in conservative repose, winding their way back to the beginning, or represent the beginning themselves. There's freedom, sure—in the blowing, the light, the wild propagation along the crest of the acre, all the beautiful kinds. But it's illusory when I really think about it. Every part suggests formation, every part is reaching home.

CHAPTER 8 \\\\

FAMILY LIFE IS PUNCTUATED BY business dinners, where the entire family entertains Baba's American colleagues from the hospital and elsewhere. The point is to impress them by being a good family. Sometimes the dinners are held outside the home, in restaurants, where Little Seed has learned to be savvy about how to behave. In Western restaurants, she wears a dress with white stockings and sits politely with a napkin on her lap all night and pretends to listen to adults. In Chinese restaurants, she wears the sweatshirt with a dog patch and sneaks under the tablecloth halfway through dinner and curls up by Mama's feet to nap.

When business dinners are at home, entire weeks are eaten up in preparation. Baba ponders the menu, considering the weather, the season, the guests' preferences. They drive an hour away to retrieve Chinese vegetables and fish from the closest Asian grocer. *Do they know how to eat eggplant?* Mama asks. *Do they know how to eat fish?* Baba expects six cold dishes on the long cherry table when guests arrive—little dishes of daikon, cucumber, eggplant, peanuts, anchovies. Shortly after guests are seated, a clear soup is served, then a stir-fry of poultry or pork, a green wilted at high heat with garlic cloves, and a whole head-on fish, steamed with ginger and scallions. The plates are cleared, and a mountain of fried rice on a platter arrives. And for dessert, something Western: a lemon curd pie or freshly baked pound cake piled high with whipped cream. (This is the traditional Chinese way of honoring guests.)

Baba's business associates have been very good to him, so it's only right to invite them for dinner to show his appreciation. *We are Chinese; that's what we do*, Mama tells Little Seed. *And anyway, they've never eaten real Chinese food, so it's our duty to let them try it*, she says. But Mama spends days and nights slicing peppers and radishes and onions and marinating meats and scaling rainbow trout. She says Baba is too busy with work to help. Mama tells Little Seed the same story again and again. *I always hated cooking*, she says. *I was the last of my sisters anyone would ever expect to learn how to cook*. Mama picks out stacks of nice white porcelain from the cabinet and counts silver out in piles on the table. *I was a musician, I was a composer and a director, I was a teacher, I was a profligate spender! I couldn't make it down Nanjing Lu without buying a Mylar bag of sour plums. I'd get home with my face and hands sticky and no plums*. She spreads a baby-pink tablecloth over the long table. *I was the one who was always rushing out in front to be number one, to fight with people when I thought they were being unfair. I was a heroine*, Mama says, softly. She cuts flowers and arranges them in a glass vase, places all the table settings. *But what I really, really, really hated was cooking!*

So why do you do it? Little Seed asks, and Mama looks up at her, holding a crystal drinking glass above a guest's setting. She ponders the question for a moment. *It's my job, and I care about doing a good job.* She sets the glass down. *And anyway, who else is going to do it?*

Baba arranges a business dinner at home before Big Brother leaves for boot camp. This dinner marks the last time they will be a family in this particular way. Little Seed puts on her Mary Janes with resolve, brushes off the lacy cuffs of her favorite dress. *This time it's serious*, she thinks, pulling tight her ponytail, which Mama has curled and adorned with a red bow. She walks out the door and onto the balcony to wait for the guests to arrive, for the opportunity to help them to be a good family, to be real in the eyes of the outside world.

BABA'S COLLEAGUE, A SERIOUS WHITE MAN in a baggy gray suit, and his wife, a woman with brassy hair who wears a navy blazer with angular shoulder pads, sit next to each other on the long end of the dinner table. Baba sits at the head, next to the man, and Little Seed and Big Brother face the couple on the opposite long side of the table. Mama is in the kitchen, wearing sweats and a drooping toque that Baba has bought her to keep strands of her hair from falling into the food. She is stirring a whisked egg into a broth of chicken bones and ginger that she has simmered overnight, and she plates the soup into delicate white bowls, floating a perfect floret of cilantro on each meniscus.

In the dining room, Baba makes eye contact with Big Brother, who wears a white tuxedo with a black bow tie and black cummerbund. On cue, Big Brother stands up, retrieves a crystal pitcher from the center of the table, and bends gracefully by the left ear of each guest to fill their water glasses, before circling around to fill the rest, just as Baba coached him to. Little Seed watches and kicks her feet under the table impatiently and concentrates—her job is to be quiet, stay still, and smile.

As Big Brother fills glasses, Baba and his colleague, a cardiologist, discuss their work at the hospital. They drink Scotch out of diamond-patterned glasses that Baba has poured on their arrival, and the white man's face is red and splotchy. His wife listens to them and seems bored, or uncomfortable, or maybe both.

"They're coming in and ruining this town, Doctor. You're not from around here, so you deserve to hear it from me," the man says. "I don't have anything against them, *truly.*" The man draws this last Southern vowel out like cream. "But you see how they line up outside the grocery store, and all their women keep havin' babies even though they're on welfare and the daddies won't stay." The man looks at Baba, his face simultaneously pleading and chiding. Is he looking for approval, or is he daring Baba to agree?

"I tell you," Baba begins, slowly, "you're not wrong, but it's not all of them." The man sobers for a moment, and he presses his hand to his mouth, blinks hard. Baba continues, "It's just the ones here who are so dumb. They're the ones who couldn't run fast enough in Africa to escape!" Baba lands the punch line with sparkling eyes, and the white man's face erupts in laughter. He coughs. He wipes tears from his bloodshot eyes.

"No, I'm not joking, I'm not joking." Baba smiles and nods, searching the man and the man's wife's face, with a grin. Little Seed heard a previous white guest tell this joke and marvels at the speed at which Baba has scavenged it.

"You're really one of us, Doctor. You get it," the man says. "You work hard, you know your place. I've never met any other Chinese like you," he goes on. Baba beams.

"We aren't like other Chinese—it's true, you know," Baba

says, looking to Big Brother and then to Little Seed, continuing to smile.

Mama pushes through the door and sets a porcelain bowl of fish maw soup in front of each guest. As they drink the delicate broth, she returns, placing platters of food one by one in a row down the center of the dining table: sweet garlic prawns, New York strip fried with peppers, chrysanthemum greens oil-slick, eggs scrambled with dried scallops. The wife asks if she can give Mama a hand, but Mama has disappeared back into the kitchen to start frying rice.

"Mama says that Chinese dishes have to be served hot," Little Seed says, apologetically, to the wife. "That's why she has to be in the kitchen." Then, Little Seed folds her napkin expertly and scoots out. She places the equilateral triangle of the napkin on the seat of her chair as she stands as straight as she can, then places her two hands on the back of the chair, pushing it in, and makes eye contact with the wife.

"Madame," Little Seed announces, self-consciously performing all the choreography Baba requires, "may I use the ladies' room?" Relief pours over her as she finishes her lines.

"Of course," the wife says, frowning slightly. Little Seed runs to the bathroom for a moment of relief away from the dinner. When she comes back, Big Brother is filling glasses again and helping to clear the half-empty platters of food while Mama delivers a final enormous platter of fried rice, to the couple's cries of awe at such abundance, such decadence.

Mama leaves the dining room again, and Baba's colleague remarks on how wonderful she is, what a wonderful wife, so patient and generous and such a good cook. He looks to his wife as he says this, to tease her. She rolls her eyes and smirks. A little later, Mama slips into her seat at the end of the table, opposite Baba, fully transformed and wearing a silk wrap dress, her face fresh and lips painted red, her hair set in curls. She smiles at everyone sweetly.

"I was just saying how wonderful you are to the doctor here," the man says, slowly, sounding out each word.

"Ahh, thank you," Mama says in carefully practiced English, smiling big and drawing the words out as if she is bowing.

"She is the best wife, it's true. She is so sweet," Baba says, beaming, his eyes soft. "But I am nothing in her eyes. You cannot even believe it! She never even notices me." He frowns clownishly. Baba's colleague and his wife smile, charmed by Baba's playfully sorry routine. That can't be true, their expressions say, and Baba shakes his head. "No, no, it's true." He points at Mama, then raises his index finger.

"Number one is her son," he says, without breaking eye contact with the man and his wife. Big Brother grimaces at the table, forces a little smile. "Number two, her daughter. Then, number three, the dog." Baba raises two more fingers, counting. At this, they both start giggling.

"Number four, my daughter's hermit crabs." Now Little Seed is laughing, and Big Brother too, if only to follow along. "Number five, the cactus in the living room." Baba extends his entire right hand for the count, and now Mama is laughing too, cautiously, her eyes watching Baba.

"And then, last place, number six, is me," Baba says, still feigning seriousness at the guests, and raising the index finger on his other hand, both hands now facing outward, as if in supplication. The guests roar with laughter at this final tally. Barely audible, the laughter from Big Brother, Little Seed, and Mama runs thin.

"So, you see, it's very hard for me," Baba says. "Stop, stop," the man says. He is crying with laughter. "You're killing me," he says. "I slave away, and it doesn't matter!" Baba says, beaming at his own performance. The room quiets again, the guests taking deep breaths.

"Well, you have two beautiful children," the wife says, turning the room's attention to Mama.

"Thank you," Mama says, smiling genuinely. "You know, you maybe can't believe, but when I come here and have my daughter, I'm forty-three." Mama punctuates the revelation with wide eyes to make her emotion clear—her triumph, her luck, her strength, and perhaps her destiny. Her body's ability to have Little Seed at such a late age means something about belonging in this new country, about deserving.

"Oh, that's amazing," the wife says, nodding furiously. "But you mustn't feel ashamed at all, having a child at that age," she says softly, considering each word. "I mean, it's what all the modern ladies are doing." She winks at Mama and flashes a smile. Mama smiles back and demurs, her eyes as empty as English.

The mood of the dinner slows down as everyone grows tired from eating and chatting. Big Brother takes his cue and steps out of the room to retrieve the pot of coffee.

AS SOON AS THE GUESTS HAVE GONE, Little Seed dashes out of her dress and into one of Big Brother's oversized T-shirts as Mama and Big Brother clear the table and stack plates in the dishwasher. Later, she scrambles into the family room and into the well-worn dent of a pink beanbag chair. Baba and Mama and Big Brother lounge quietly on beat-up leather couches and a massage chair next to a gas fire.

Everyone is content; they can relax now that they have, as

a family, shown the guests a wonderful night. Baba sits back in his recliner, tranquil as a cat, reading a newspaper, and begins imagining out loud the future beyond their front door.

After Big Brother becomes big and strong in the Navy, he will go to medical school at Harvard and become a brilliant doctor who travels the world healing people from different parts of the world.

For a little while, he will take a sabbatical in London, where he will own a town house filled with books and exotic plants. Every night, there is a glamorous cocktail party for him to attend, wearing tails and a top hat. It's there that he meets a lady friend, and his future wife, a royal heiress with whom he will clink glasses of Dom Perignon. He'll return home to America with his new wife, and a British accent, and he'll eventually grow so wealthy that Little Seed will never have to work a day in her life.

How many children will you have, Big Brother? Baba asks, peeking over the leaves of his newspaper. *Two or three?*

Little Seed looks to Big Brother, imagining this life, and feeling reassured that even this new wrinkle of the Navy won't disrupt the expansiveness of his future—if Baba says it's true, it must be true. Big Brother returns Baba's mischievous smile.

No, Big Brother says. *I want five children*, he answers tentatively, studying the carpet, glancing up at Baba. Baba smiles and Little Seed smiles too, pulling a stuffed rabbit to her chest.

Wait, says Big Brother sharply, and Mama, Baba, and Little Seed look at him. *I want eight*, he says.

No! Twelve! Mama laughs, and Little Seed collapses into giggles, thinking of all the babies as she tugs lovingly at the rabbit's ears.

This cosmos of sofas and soft light, so rich in possibility, as pliant as a daydream, permeates each of them, simultaneously reaching through the past and into the future, as the streetlights just outside the casement windows begin to turn on, one after another. The outside world goes black, the shadows grow long and strange, but the universe in this home coils around itself into increasingly sophisticated designs. It speaks its own language, devises its own order, grows stronger despite all that lies on the other side of the front door. Security is just the cleverness of a load-bearing wall, safety just blending in. It's a wonder that, looking in from the street, you wouldn't know the difference between this place and any other place at all.

II. NAMES

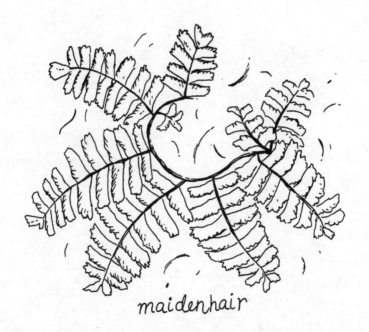

maidenhair

LITTLE SEED AND MAMA FLY to Chicago to attend Big Brother's graduation from boot camp. It's the only time they will ever take a trip without Baba, because Baba won't allow it. While Mama is gone, Baba says he can't sleep and won't eat and whimpers constantly about his ranking in Mama's affections, how he is in last place, how she cares only about Big Brother. Overhearing the childlike softness of his voice through the landline of the hotel, Little Seed remembers the brawls Baba and Big Brother used to have on the family room floor, wrestling like children on the carpet. It would always start playfully enough, then Big Brother would knee Baba, and Baba would bite Big Brother, and Mama would have to break them up. What would have happened if she didn't? Was this *Chinese*?

Home without Big Brother has been shrunken and quiet.

Baba's anger and jealousy over Mama's affection for Big Brother abates. He is now able to colonize all of her attention. Mama says Baba isn't as jealous of Little Seed because she is a girl. An iciness persists between her parents. Without Big Brother to reassure her or to take her into the world to play, Little Seed absorbs the melancholy in the house and wilts, spending more and more time alone. What is she supposed to do without Big Brother to guide her?

But in Chicago, Little Seed and Mama are both invigorated, knowing they'll get to see Big Brother again. They are on an adventure together, traversing a foreign world of snow and skyscrapers to get to Big Brother, the winter air bracing in their throats. They are joined against the outside world. When they arrive at the hotel, Mama brandishes a credit card and tells the clerk that she'd like to reserve a room in addition to theirs, for Big Brother to sleep in by himself, and Little Seed can tell she has been practicing these lines from her steady concentration, how her voice goes a little lower, how she courageously maintains eye contact as she speaks.

She explains to Little Seed that Big Brother has suffered too much for the past eight weeks in training and deserves this small luxury, and Little Seed is surprised to hear about unhappiness. When she speaks to him on the phone, he makes her laugh by impersonating his captain, who screams until his face is red if his shoes are not polished to high shine. She knows about the creaky bunk beds, the friends he says he is making, the pranks they pull on one another. To her, they are exotic: there's Chris, whose family is Pennsylvania Dutch, and Carl, a lifelong vegetarian who occasionally gets mistaken for Leonardo DiCaprio. Big Brother doesn't tell her about the exhaustion and the fear, how the toilet seats are confiscated so recruits can't hang themselves during training.

The clerk asks Mama if she needs to hire a car to and from the graduation ceremony and shows her a list of options on a laminated piece of paper. Mama points confidently to the most expensive item on the list, a white stretch limousine, and Little Seed squeezes Mama's hand out of excitement, imagining how glamorous it will be and how happy it will make Big Brother.

The ceremony is set in an enormous gymnasium. Little Seed and Mama sit in the front row, and after the national anthem plays and the flag is presented, they watch as men and women in dark uniforms and white garrison caps file into the space and march in rows around the gymnasium. It is strange to observe so many expressionless faces in unison, staring ahead, the small muscles of their arms and legs coordinated perfectly. There is wordless shouting, the roar of voices flattened by the relentless cascade of footsteps against the wooden floor.

Little Seed picks out Big Brother, finally. She looks at Mama, who sees him too and is smiling and wiping her eyes. As Big Brother approaches, Little Seed waves and shouts his name, tipping forward out of her seat in impatience. But Big Brother remains in his role, his face drawn and serious. Suddenly, all the soldiers extend their right arms. Their hands are clutching roses, and they march up the bleachers to their respective family members. Big Brother offers his roses to Little Seed with a brief encouraging glance; she feels relieved to be seen by him and takes the flowers, which are made of plastic and polyester. She touches the red petals that have been sewn together in spiraling layers, plastic teardrops glued to the outermost edges to resemble morning dew. When she looks up again, Big Brother's gaze has retreated back into the organism of dark uniforms.

The limousine feels empty on the way back to the hotel, after the ceremony. Little Seed observes snowdrifts on the side of the streets, the empty crystal decanter and ornate glass tumblers lining the doors of the car. Behind the partition, the black leather seats face each other, and Mama attempts to make small talk with Big Brother, asking him what he misses eating the most, what he'd like to do before he has to return back to his base the next day, searching for a need or a desire she can fulfill. Little Seed feels annoyed at her desperate reaching. Will there be any attention left for her? But Big Brother is far away, nodding vaguely and answering in short sentences. Little Seed feels that the remove of his voice and his distraction are an unbearable chasm. She tries to traverse it, by attempting to make him laugh, by telling him stories about her new classmates, her own new friends. If only she can persuade him to come back to her, she can ask him why things at home are so strange, what she's supposed to do about it. But he smiles weakly at her and turns away to stare out the window, where strangers are bundled up in enormous down coats and knit hats, going home to other families and other lives.

SOON, MAMA BEGINS TO DIE. It happens unpredictably. She becomes furious at Little Seed for making a mess of her room, or for doing poorly in school, or for being lazy at practicing piano. Is it a punishment? Little Seed becomes fearful of blame and defeated, conscious that Mama's judgment of her, no matter how contained and reasonable at first, might tumble into mania. When the boundary is crossed, Little Seed's world shrinks to the two of them, every ripple an earthquake.

Mama's eyes bulge, she pulls the face of her skin taut into a menacing frown, and her words turn into sirens. *Little Seed is an ungrateful, selfish child. She is wicked and only wants and wants and wants. Where did she even learn such greed?* Surely it must be from the outside, Little Seed thinks. Surely it must be because she is American and not fully Chinese like the rest of her family.

I hope you have a daughter as evil as you are one day. But Mama must be the most evil that Little Seed should be like this. Mama should just die. If she would go and just die, everyone else would be happy. Little Seed can't see from crying. Then, when Mama stops yelling completely, Little Seed feels a premature relief.

Mama has collapsed, her head slack against the tank of the toilet in the guest bathroom, or the velvet cushions of the sofa, or the kitchen floor. Her mouth is open and her eyelids reveal two glassy half-moons of white. Her shoulders slump back, her cheek is pressed against the floor, and the late-afternoon light (these tantrums seem to occur only in perfect light) is crisp on her face, pale as the moon, the skin soft and freckled, the curls of her short hair hanging loosely.

Little Seed falls into her lap, screaming. She swears over and over that she will be good if only Mama will wake up, unsure if she will. If she doesn't, she knows that it will be because Little Seed has been selfish. She resolves to be as careful as she can by making herself small enough for there to be no mistakes, no uncertainties, to never hurt Mama again.

There is a breeze from the window above the toilet. Little Seed's eyes feel hot and painful. She presses her face against Mama's legs, frightened of what Baba and Big Brother might think if they saw her there, frightened to think that she is the one, in the end—not Baba or Big Brother—who has destroyed her family.

Please don't die, Little Seed chants softly. *Please don't die.* She wonders how a moment can possibly be so large. The child part of her disappears each time she grows to contain Mama, to attempt to revive her through wishes, whimpering into her icy, limp fingers.

Mama stirs, finally, her eyes fluttering open, and Little Seed looks at her in fear and relief. Mama's face is emotionless, bewildered and drained of color, and Little Seed understands that she can never tell Baba or Big Brother what has happened. She must protect both of them now and forever. She will contain Mama's pain over and over again, even after she grows up and leaves. Is this what it means to be filial? Is this what it means to be *Chinese*?

Mama turns her head slowly to look at Little Seed and instructs her to wet a towel with cold water and bring it to her, and Little Seed frantically obliges, turning on the sink and watching the water seep into the white terry cloth and turn it gray. She offers the towel to Mama, whose gaze is still distant.

See what happens when you are bad? Mama says softly, taking the cool towel from Little Seed's hands and pressing it to her forehead. Little Seed watches, her hands still outstretched, her mind too blank with terror to do anything but cling to the fine lines of Mama's face, how they shift through different expressions over the course of a minute. (How easy it would be for Mama to hug her or to reassure her, to remind Little Seed that she is only a child.) Little Seed is just skin and the weight of her body as she watches Mama stand up. Her heart and her mind have coalesced entirely on Mama's slim body, on her slumping shoulders, on her legs as they stretch and step slowly. (There is still time for her to come to Little Seed and wipe the tears from her face. There is still time to teach Little Seed that what Mama wants or needs needn't render Little Seed invisible.) Mama lingers, just long enough to change her mind, then leaves.

LITTLE SEED HAS NO CHOICE except to go outside, even if it frightens her. She has stopped hoping for home to be safe without Big Brother. The woods just beyond her home are filled with curiosities—grasshoppers the size of her hand, painted in autumn colors, that launch themselves into flight from her fingertips, watermelon bugs that curl up languorously into perfect marbles.

Up and down the forest, baby-pink wildflowers emerge from rock piles. She gathers and dries them along an old stone wall behind the house. She's making potions, wishing for the days to be shorter so Big Brother can visit her, or at least for the distance she experienced in Chicago to dissipate. She knows the Navy, cast upon him like a spell, must be to blame for it. She learns to stretch long blades of grass between her fingers and blow through them to whistle. She climbs a tulip poplar, watching the forest from its branches. And though she is not allowed in the creaking barn behind her house, she sneaks in and watches the sun freeze dust and dirt in midair. Years pass in this uneasy outdoor freedom. She meanders around the forest, waiting for Big Brother to come back to her.

One day a teacher gives her a jar filled with three tadpoles captured in a creek—they are forest green, fat thumbs attached to wisps of tail. Little Seed watches each day as they circle one another in the glass. Day by day, their tails shorten and they grow arms and legs, each limb articulated in segments.

The last feature to define itself is the head, the eyes appearing like small beads, and Little Seed is frightened to see this, that they have suddenly become frogs, real animals now that seem to be able to regard her. She panics, imagining that they might drown in the water, and rushes to pour them out in the backyard, forcing herself not to wonder what happens from there, where they will go, if they will continue to live.

CHAPTER 10 \\\\ Maidenhair and Bracken

THE RESURRECTION FERN, or *Pleopeltis polypodioides*, possesses a mechanism that allows it to die and come back each spring. The fern is common throughout the Southeast, and though I can't remember noticing it when I was little, I must have brushed past its colonies, which rise like cockscomb on rocks and the rough bark of trees, their pinnae covered in fuzzy gray scales. During dry spells in the late summer, the fern withers and grows brittle. But this desiccated state keeps the fern alive under blankets of winter snow. The fern holds on to just enough water and waits for the next storm.

The resurrection fern shares its colloquial name with another fern: *Selaginella lepidophylla*, a Mexican desert species that resembles a tumbleweed in arid conditions. It's commonly known as a resurrection plant. In rain or in shallow water, it reabsorbs moisture, blooming and becoming vivid green. It's sometimes also called the flower of stone or the Jericho rose. Or in Spanish, *siempre viva*. In Mexico, the water used to soak a resurrection plant is given to women to help initiate labor— and the quickness with which the ball of twigs unwinds into green fronds forecasts the ease of birth.

I like that these two ferns share a colloquial name as well as a way of being, and I also like that (as with all species) they have permanent Latin names too, so I can be certain which is which. It's a string I can keep tugging on to reach my destination, no matter how long it takes, no matter how lost I get.

NAMES, FOR ME, USE CERTAINTY as their lure. They're above and beneath us, a universal interface, a boulder fastened to the earth. I don't have a head for figures or order or permanence, but it soothes me to know that *somebody* does.

What I want is a heavy book I can flip through to find the name of anything I don't recognize, the name of the thing rendered in a dead language so I can know that I won't be wrong, no matter who is looking. I know that everything is up for interpretation, but maybe some things aren't, and that's for the best. Ferns grow regardless of our opinion of them. They spiral relentlessly.

Let me tell you something soothing: Everything alive exists in three categories called Domains, and within that, five or six of seven divisions called Kingdoms (depending on the zoologist you're speaking with). All plants, including ferns, exist in the one called Plantae. No matter what language you speak, these names remain the same.

It gets messy up close, but only for the sake of precision: ferns have been classified and reclassified again and again, split apart and put back together, whenever scientists learn more. They first started out in a class called Filices and later moved to the division Pteridophyta, for vascular plants that reproduce using spores. The division Pteridophyta was retired when phylogeneticists discovered that some pteridophytes are closer, evolutionarily speaking, to some angiosperms than to the other ferns. Those were reclassified as fern allies (more on this later) and later officially moved to their own class called Lycopodiopsida. The rest of the ferns were reassigned to the division Polypodiophyta, within which exist four extant families of ferns.

Still, scientists are diligent about assigning a genus and species to each variety of fern, and so far, they've assigned about 210 genera and around 10,000 species names. Like Chinese names, we address them first by their broader genus, then by their individual species, in Latin or Greek, or words stretched to sound Latin or Greek: *Athyrium filix-femina. Adiantum capillus-veneris. Dryopteris pulcherrima. Osmunda japonica.* First they belong, then they stray.

IT MIGHT SEEM CHALLENGING to understand what separates the species of ferns into genera, but I can help, at least a little.

Maidenhairs are one of the easiest genera to know. Their genus is *Adiantum*, which comes from the Greek word "unwetted," which refers to the way water is shed from their pinnules. They are coveted as houseplants because they are classically delicate. They can also be difficult to maintain, given their requirement for humid and low-lit places. In nature, you find them trailing over river rocks or spilling down the crests of waterfalls. Their pinnules look like heavily lashed eyelids or folding fans and hover from dark, fine stipes. From far away they are inkblots suspended in the air. Sori develop on the back of the tips of their pinnules, covered by papery indusia that make their edges look dog-eared.

Some *Adiantum* are fleetingly pink: the comblike pinnae of *Adiantum hispidulum*, the rosy maidenhair fern, for instance, are fuchsia when young, then turn deep green later. The fronds grow radially in clusters of five, so new growths appear among older fronds, like starfish in seaweed. The sky-pink pinnules of the large-leaf fern, or *Adiantum macrophyllum*, are oversized diamonds that fan out down the length of the stipe. The color fades away slowly, like a burn receding, until just a blush thumbprint remains.

BRACKEN, OR *PTERIDIUM*, is a genus of fern that is as easy to recognize as maidenhair for its distinct appearance and also for its commonness and international distribution: where there are people, there is bracken. Compared to fussy maidenhair, bracken is virulent, growing in a vast range of conditions from sandy soils to pastures, thriving without much rainfall. Its fronds are coarse and leathery, lacking lace or air; the enormous triangles splay out in a single plane high above the ground on woody stems, sometimes as tall as a person. The pinnae develop an ultimate pinnule at their apex that grows twice as long as the others. This ultimate growth usually absorbs adjoining pinnules imprecisely, so that the perimeter of this ultimate pinnule looks like a messy sketch. In fall, sori trace the perimeter of the back of each pinna, like an unbroken line of golden embroidery. Its hardiness and propensity to overgrow and inhibit native plant species make bracken extremely adaptable, and as a result the genus is considered by humans to be weedy and invasive.

The fiddleheads and fronds of *Pteridium* contain the toxic enzyme thiaminase, which, in large doses, is poisonous to humans and ruminants. Bracken consumption can be fatal to horses, which exhibit difficulty standing, back legs bracing as though saddled with a heavy weight.

I hold maidenhair and bracken in my mind as opposites: what is ethereal and lovely versus what is hulking and dangerous. But I don't always look closely enough; I don't always have the capacity to go deeper. Wild, untidy bracken often supports a universe of tiny beings within its cool, dark shade, organisms that can't survive being trampled: tiny bluebells, white stars of wood anemone, and certain mosses are able to thrive in the safety and the humidity cultivated within their vast stands. The yellowleg bonnet, *Mycena epipterygia*, is sometimes found living under the large leaves of bracken. Its delicate, glassy caps perch on thin, yellow stems, and its mycelia, tangled thick underground, glow green in the dark.

CHAPTER 11 \\\

AFTER SIX YEARS IN THE NAVY, Big Brother enrolls in college again, at a small liberal arts school in Pennsylvania. He decides, on his own, to go premed. Mama and Baba can breathe again, now that his life is on the right track and their sacrifices won't be for nothing. He is six years older than his peers but sends Little Seed photographs of himself barbecuing with his friends, packages of books he's read, with names like *The Waste Land and Other Poems* and *The Iliad*, whose English is indecipherable to her. Little Seed feels intimidated by the books Big Brother gives her, but she chooses, also, to feel full in his renewed attention. Big Brother's disconnection from her was temporary. All of her waiting was worth it. She'll work hard until she can read the books, until they can be her favorites too.

At Big Brother's urging, Mama and Baba decide to send Little Seed to boarding school. He tells them that the wealthy white teenagers that have become his friends at college have all matriculated through a tangled network of private schools along the East Coast where they became cultured and well-spoken. They dressed and moved differently than the less well-off students. They were treated better. And anyway, Mama and Baba are rich now. In the six years that Big Brother spent in the Navy, they started a successful clinic together in Tennessee. Shouldn't they invest in the type of education that will help Little Seed go anywhere she wants?

Big Brother locates a boarding school an hour from home, in Asheville, and submits applications for Little Seed to enroll immediately, for her first year of high school. Little Seed feels frightened but is bolstered by the thought that Big Brother is looking out for her. If this is the direction his attention leads, she will follow. Mama is reluctant, even after Little Seed is accepted into the school. She meets with the headmaster, who really does wear tweeds and horn-rimmed glasses. She expresses her concern that Little Seed is becoming rough and unsophisticated, playing alone every day in their narrow strip of woods. "Don't worry," he says, touching her lightly on the arm. "After four years here, she'll be an entirely different person."

WHAT LITTLE SEED LIKES THE MOST are the Delta Blondes. There are four or five of them on campus, and they each have double names like Mary Louise or Emma Archer and speak in cultured Southern drawls and darting glances. They are from Mississippi or Alabama, and some of the other students make furtive jokes about how they come from plantation money, how their families owned slaves. These facts only serve to make them more interesting to Little Seed, who imagines glittering aristocratic pasts.

They wear Manolo Blahnik stilettos and muted Chanel sets to class and keep to themselves. They seem mature and self-possessed, their mascara and blush perfectly applied, their hair glittering in the sun. Envy consumes her like fire: she is totally unlike them.

She can't imagine them crying night after night in their dorm rooms as they fall asleep, missing a home they are frightened of but cannot leave, fearful of every new thing they encounter. She can't imagine them hating themselves for knowing so little about American culture—the right food, the right music, the right beaches where one's family is supposed to spend the summer. How can it matter so much whether it's Hilton Head or St. Simons? She can't imagine them copying the phrases and facts and personalities of their peers, making up a new face. They seem to know everything already. They know so much it doesn't even occur to them to care about looking like they know. They do what they want, guided only by their desires and the ticking hours of the day. They are the most beautiful girls Little Seed has ever seen.

LITTLE SEED LEARNS TO MANEUVER. Her first friends at school are gawky middle-class girls from the Midwest. When they first arrive, they bond over how alienated they feel by their refined peers, and though Little Seed likes them, she dislikes being relegated to the fringes of the student body. She dreams of change and invention. Her friends wear ill-fitting blazers and cheap, pilling sweaters and don't seem to yearn to become better liked. They are uninterested in the Delta Blondes.

Little Seed begins to understand that there is an unspoken

code to dressing. All the stylish white girls stick together and speak in a different language peppered with vocabulary that Little Seed is desperate to absorb—Neiman Marcus, Saks Fifth Avenue, Barneys, Bergdorf, Bendel's. (The Delta Blondes are the most rarefied species within this genus of girl.) She demands that her parents buy her an enormous collection of shoes, explaining that the other girls have so many and it is embarrassing for her not to have them too. Mama and Baba are susceptible, Little Seed learns, to the anxiety that others might look down on her. Little Seed comes to love shoes, or at least the idea of loving shoes: she collects designer mules, wedges, and boots wrapped in blue taffeta, lambskin, cowhide. She has a pair of knee-high suede stiletto boots with striped leather up the back. She has peep-toe pumps in red crocodile.

Piece by piece, she builds a common language with the stylish white girls and makes herself less available to the awkward middle-class girls. When they do visit her room, she lets them look through her collection of shoes and is relieved to know that the $600 label on a pair of Marc Jacobs pumps establishes an irreparable distance between them. The stylish white girls begin inviting her to spend the hour after study hall with them in their rooms. They discuss, among other topics, how loathsome the unstylish girls are.

It is impossible for Little Seed not to notice that the annoying and gross girls also contain the other girls who are not white, save for the only other Asian American girl at the school, a Vietnamese adoptee who speaks with a thick Kentucky accent. Little Seed is horribly jealous of her place on the volleyball team, her handsome white boyfriend, her inexplicable and easy friendship with the Delta Blondes. Though their races are not mentioned explicitly in the nightly summits, it is clear that it is undesirable to be aligned with the girls who are Jewish, or Black, or Latina, or international, or ethnically ambiguous, or poor, or awkward, or weird. Little Seed understands that she must comply with these boundaries if she wants access to this room. For Little Seed, friendship is about learning to become herself by binding herself to those whom she thinks she wants to be.

The stylish white girls invite Little Seed to have dinner with them one night, and one of the girls (brunette, a pink fitted polo, a silk headband) makes a joke about their collective whiteness. Little Seed laughs along, and the same girl stops the conversation, waving her hand furiously. She points out that Little Seed is, in fact, not white, and all the girls erupt into laughter. Are they laughing at Little Seed's willful racial amnesia? Are they laughing at their own? Little Seed laughs as hard as anyone.

CHAPTER 12 \\\\ Forest Ferns

WE ONCE PROJECTED STORIES of ourselves, of ascendance, onto ferns. The Victorians ascribed anxieties of dominance and need into the structures of ferns. Since ferns don't produce flowers, it was said that only those with the most sophisticated taste might appreciate the hidden elegance and subtle beauty of a fern. The act of hunting for ferns could be taken on only by those with keen intelligence and observational prowess. And you might judge a person's refinement by the selection of species in their gardens.

This feels familiar, of course—social acceptance via tones and postures, a private language for everyone who possesses an ease and elegance you don't. Look at a fern and say that you register the same beauty in a frond as in a shock of wildflowers in a field or in the sudden change in autumn of maple leaves from green to scarlet: appreciate the fern. Or at least lie.

I wonder about the ceiling on such affectations. Surely there was a limit to the return such social climbing could win you. Maybe someone unfashionable and awkward could win a single invitation to a salon by deciphering a maidenhair fern from bracken. But if they tried to capitalize on the moiety of grace their fact-finding has won them by becoming encyclopedic in their knowledge of genera and species, they risk becoming annoying, the fern girl who won't shut up about ferns after everyone else has moved on to more interesting things, like whether or not it's appropriate to leave your piano legs uncovered. (The Victorians!)

I'd still want to become fluent in ferns, in spite of potential social reward or social alienation. And anyway, I find learning the names of genera and species to be tranquilizing. It's as if scientists filled a filing cabinet with forest. If I can just be diligent enough, I'll always be able to locate every blade, sorus, and fiddlehead. Nothing will ever go missing.

DRYOPTERIS IS ONE OF the largest genera of ferns, containing four hundred species. They are colloquially known as wood ferns and are commonly found in forests. Think of a fern: your mind's eye calls up *Dryopteris*. Their pinnae are heavily subdivided, often bright green against the forest floor. Their sori are round and numerous, an alien bubble sheet. Pinned on each sorus is a kidney-shaped indusium, dimpled at its center.

Of the eleven species of *Dryopteris* on the East Coast, the largest is the evergreen wood fern, *Dryopteris intermedia*, whose fronds can grow up to three feet in length. The smallest is the fragrant cliff fern, *Dryopteris fragrans*, which makes its home in north-facing cliffs and outcrops of limestone. As its fronds wither and die, they hang from the base of the plant for several years, stitching together a sienna curtain for newly green fronds to grow against. The new leaves smell sweetly of primrose.

Given their classic fernlike appearances, Dryopteris ferns are often grown as ornamentals. *Dryopteris erythrosora*, or autumn fern, is a favorite in gardens. Its large fiddleheads are rose-colored and unravel into enormous copper fronds every fall. Another species common to gardens is the male fern, *Dryopteris filix-mas*, which botanical texts are always praising for its erectness and vigor, for its uprightness—it's said that its fiddleheads resemble a man's fist punching through the earth. Fern literature seems wholly influenced by the fern's vernacular name, which was given sometime in the 1800s. The male fern was so named for its apparent differences with the lady fern, *Athyrium filix-femina*, which was considered small and graceful.

Unlike men and women, the two ferns have little in common, aside from their tendency to grow in compact rosettes. (Part of why they are coveted as garden ornamentals.) In the present taxonomy, they even occupy different genera. The common names persist even as our views on gender shift. The ferns capture how we perceived each other in a different time, what we meant when we cared a lot about calling ourselves and each other men and women.

An enviable thing about ferns, though, is that they remain ferns, innocent of any gendered traits projected onto them. The wispy diamond shape of a lady fern just doesn't look very much like a woman, no matter how imaginative a botanist you might be. Ferns are safe from language.

ELSEWHERE ON THE FOREST FLOOR, ferns of the genus *Asplenium*, commonly called spleenworts, are recognizable for the yearning quality of their fronds. They whip around, stretch languidly, hunt out crevices in rock. Their fronds look like spines, their pinnules stacked on top of one another. The stipes are usually wiry and dark, and their colloquial name is a good way to remember that their sori are narrow, oblong, or linear, like spleens. Underground, their rhizomes are flecked by translucent scales with fine black veins. They are said to resemble stained glass.

One interesting spleenwort is the walking fern, or *Asplenium rhizophyllum*, whose spade-shaped leaves have developed proliferous frond tips, from which new ferns can grow. As their blades mature, they bend toward the earth until their apexes touch soil, and the tips grow into new plants without separating from the parent plant. They arc around, slowly wandering the forest floor, an ongoing, unbroken connection to the previous generation.

Beech ferns, genus *Phegopteris*, are easy to recognize because the lowest pair of pinnae on their large, triangular fronds points in the opposite direction of the blade's apex, as if it is being dragged away. The broad beech fern, *Phegopteris hexagonoptera*, earned its species name because its arrangement of pinnae is geometric: if you draw straight lines connecting each point of its pinnae, the result would be a lazy hexagon. The common narrow beech fern, *Phegopteris connectilis*, has slim fronds, so the lowest pair appears to be trailing behind the rest of the frond like the wake of a boat.

Another fern of geometry is the oak fern, genus *Gymnocarpium*. Its fronds grow three pinnae, which, taken together, create the shape of an equilateral triangle. Its blades grow as individuals, rather than in clutches or rosettes, and rise up on tall, wiry stipes along meandering rhizomes. Oak fern groves play tricks on the eye; a field of their symmetrical fronds has a moiré effect, undulating even when still.

Closer to the ground, near rocks and boulders, live tiny lip ferns, genus *Cheilanthes*, which grow in tufts and are distinctive for having pinnae and stipes covered in a fine wool that helps them to draw in water, even in dry places. Their pinnules are slightly puckered, so the fronds look embossed.

Higher up in the fine crevices of rock faces and cliffs live tufts of cliff ferns, genus *Woodsia*, which are able to cling in unlikely places with their short, thick rhizomes. They exhibit a huge range of styles, from the classic feathery fronds of the blunt-lobed cliff fern, *Woodsia ilvensis*, to the short, fanlike pinnules of the smooth cliff fern, *Woodsia glabella*. With *Woodsia*, it's as if the entire universe of fern genera has been miniaturized to dwell in a parallel universe of verticality. What unites these species are their indusia, which look like tiny fists clutching sori greedily.

Easy to confuse with *Woodsia* are the bladder ferns, genus *Cystopteris*, which live in the same crevices. Bladder ferns are more likely to resemble herbs like parsley or carrot greens. Distinguishing between cliff ferns and bladder ferns generally comes down to sori: unlike cliff ferns, *Cystopteris* exhibits an indusium that looks like a small pocket or a bladder, inspiring its Latinate and common names. One species, the bulblet fern, *Cystopteris bulbifera*, develops a dozen or so bulblets that grow like a string of pearls underneath the blade—they drop when ripe and flourish on their own into new ferns.

Bladder fern species are particularly difficult to tell apart from one another, their identification often hinging on something as difficult to discern as the relative narrowness of a blade or how tapered the fronds are. Bladder ferns also hybridize easily, creating specimens that exhibit the qualities of two different species, defying identification as they continue on to reproduce with other species and sometimes other hybrids.

TOWERING ABOVE THESE FOREST FERNS are the flowering ferns, called such either because of their magnificent shuttle-cock looks or because they grow two distinct types of fronds: one that develops spores (a fertile frond) and one that doesn't (a sterile frond). The sterile fronds resemble normal fern fronds, while the fertile fronds take on more interesting designs.

The regal ostrich fern, *Matteuccia struthiopteris*, is the only species in its genus. It's large, growing several feet tall in a tidy ring, its blades arranged like a plume of that enormous bird. Its spores grow on the tops of fertile fronds at the center of the plant, like ribbon sticks. The sori resemble tangles of string beans. The pinnae of the sterile fronds are thin, tapered lances, so when rippled by wind, the fronds spin like real feathers.

In contrast, the pinnules of the sterile fronds of *Osmunda* ferns are bubbly and huge. Their fronds can grow several feet long. Their enormous fiddleheads develop quickly in spring, the crosiers swathed in white or copper wool. The sori that develop on their fertile fronds look like cracked spheres and clump to-gether like sleigh bells. The fertile fronds are the first to emerge in spring and make the ferns easy to name.

The fertile fronds of the interrupted fern, *Osmunda clay-toniana*, produce sori on pinnules only in the middle of the blade. (The apex and base of the blade produce normal leafy pinnules.) When the sori ripen and shrivel in fall, they leave a band of air in the middle of each blade, their tips and bases still green and leafy. The royal fern, *Osmunda regalis*, is one of the most enormous ferns in North America, growing up to six feet in height. Its fertile fronds resemble the interrupted fern, but with sori shriveling the tips of the blades rather than at the midsections. The fertile fronds of cinnamon ferns, *Osmunda cinnamomea*, are tall, umber wands that grow woolly with sori in autumn, as if heavy with the spice.

Cinnamon fern was very recently reclassified as genus *Osmundastrum* after genetic testing found that the fern is not as closely related to the other *Osmunda* ferns as once suspected. This is a common scenario with ferns, especially with the advent of genetic testing. I like learning about how classifications meander, how a name is true, and later, not at all—like the retired genus *Pteridophyta* or the lady ferns. You have to name something in order to begin. And even after the classification shifts, the original name remains as part of the path toward discovering what is true.

CHAPTER 13 \\\\

LITTLE SEED VISITS HOME for a weekend, and the noise is as bad as ever. Baba refuses to speak to Mama when they are all together, and at night, she hears the sound of their screaming voices drifting through the floor of her room. While she and Mama are making up her bed with clean sheets for the brief visit, Mama identifies the circulating violence.

Baba wants sex all the time, and he yells "walla walla"—like that—when I don't want to, Mama says sullenly, pulling the down comforter through a lavender duvet cover. Little Seed has not heard the Shanghainese word for *sex* before. She feels embarrassed as she watches Mama pat down the comforter, her hands focused on matching the corners precisely. She doesn't know where to look.

He says he deserves it because I'm his wife and he works so hard to provide for us. He says he is humiliated when I don't give it to him. But I hate it, it hurts, she says, giving Little Seed a pillowcase and gesturing to one of the pillows. *Maybe it is my duty, so I tell him, "Okay, so you do what I want."* Mama sits on the bed, with its perfectly aligned duvet. *"I'll just lie here like I'm a dead person,"* she says, stroking the down as if it were a docile cat.

Little Seed tugs the covers on the pillow and pretends not to listen as she considers what she is being told. If sex is what causes the persistent anger in her home, she wishes Mama would just give it to Baba and stop stoking his anger. After an entire lifetime of noise in her home, she would trade anything for peace. Mama confesses that she called Big Brother and told him too, and he had books shipped to the house, all lightly re-searched self-help about how to have a wonderful sex life well into one's sixties. Because of the package, Baba learned that Mama had revealed his outrage about sex to Big Brother, and it makes his anger exponential now that it is also tinged with jealousy.

This is the first time Mama has discussed sex with her, aside from innuendos about how Little Seed must not make a "mis-take" before she is married. Little Seed hasn't even had a kiss yet, though she is eager about it. She is curious about boys, finds herself having exhilarating crushes. It's a relief that being home is only temporary now. If she can manage to tolerate it for just a few days, she'll be far away at boarding school again. She is sixteen and hasn't had the space yet to consider her body in relation to another body, how she wants to be touched, how she wants to be seen, though of course she knows that whirl-wind of light in her body, when she is alone. But she is chas-tened by this early definition of sex between people, sex as vi-olence and as a token exchanged for peace.

When you get married, Mama says, raising her gaze from the bed as Little Seed stacks the finished pillows neatly at its head, *be sure to marry someone ten years or older than you.* Little Seed stares at her, rapt at the topic of romance.

That's what your grandmother did, Mama continues. *When you get older and stop wanting it, they are much older too and also stop wanting it. Men keep wanting it much longer than women do. It's more natural this way*, she says. Little Seed recoils hearing this, the calculation simultaneously so pragmatic and so crass. She desperately attempts to divide the excitement she feels about romance and marriage from the anger and disgust she feels about her parents' sex life. But they are now inevitably linked in her mind, and the only thing she can really feel is the distress Mama radiates, sitting motionless on the bed, eyes lost in the duvet. Little Seed paces around the bed, patting down the duvet, pulling on the sheets, and arranging the pillows until they're tidy.

BY AUTUMN, MAMA TELLS LITTLE SEED, by phone, that things are better and she has learned to tolerate Baba's requests for sex. She says that she saw a photograph that Little Seed posted to her LiveJournal, of two children holding hands and roller-skating, and that it inspired her to learn to be like that with Baba. Like two children playing together? Little Seed wonders, feeling unnerved by her mother's interpretation of a thing that she feels is entirely for herself. Mama tells Little Seed that it's up to Mama to learn to like it.

Soon after, Mama and Baba pick her up for Thanksgiving break, her first holiday away from school, and she is relieved not to have to hear about sex between her parents. They let her practice driving, and she winds along the highway through the changing Blue Ridge Mountains, shrouded in a mist that mutes the reds and greens of the forest, blurring together the waning summer green. It is as if they are underwater.

When they turn onto the street of their home, Little Seed notices Big Brother's car in the driveway. By now she has stopped expecting him to come home, after so many years that he has chosen, instead, to travel or to stay with his friends' families. She has never stopped missing him, but it is easy to accept—every family reunion deteriorates into chaos and anger. Mama gasps, opens her door, and runs out into the street, grasping her purse against her side, while the car is still moving. Little Seed hits the brakes.

What's going on? she demands, turning to Baba, in the passenger seat. He looks at her, his face empty of expression. *I won't go in until you tell me*, she says.

I don't know, he says, his eyes growing soft. Little Seed stubbornly puts the car in park, in the middle of the street, as cars begin to line up behind her. He takes a deep breath. *Really, I don't know*, he says. *Come, let's go, and we'll find out together.*

In the kitchen, Big Brother sits at his usual seat at their wooden dining table. It is round and sturdy, each foot carved into a lion's head. He smiles when Little Seed enters the room, but his eyes look straight through her.

How are you doing? he says, his voice distant. *Are you enjoying school?* he ventures, his eyes like fishbowls. Little Seed thinks of the packages of books and the letters he has mailed to her over the past years, from Lhasa or Boston or France. He always reminded her to peel back the stamps to reveal the hidden messages he'd scrawled beneath them, his wild handwriting hurried and vibrant. But now, sitting across from him at the table, she can only connect the moment to the memory of sitting with him in a limousine in frigid Chicago after he'd enlisted. Why does it feel so weird?

Little Seed experiences Big Brother's recalcitrance as pure loss. She recalls how badly she has needed him to guide her, to help her make sense of their strange home. And now he's the one who is strange. Sitting with him, she's surprised to discover that she still intensely desires his guidance. How can she reconcile her need for him to continue naming the universe—what is good, what is useful, and where to go—with the strangeness of the body in front of her? Mama is whispering urgently into the landline on the wall.

Later, Mama tells Little Seed that Big Brother had been missing for a month. No one had told her because they didn't want to disrupt her studies. His advisers said he had been overwhelmed by his course load before he disappeared. He was simply under too much academic pressure. But Little Seed wonders if it is also the hour-by-hour weight of knowing and not knowing, of pushing oneself to adapt and seeing how far you can convince others of your invention.

Can you learn the brands of organic bunny cookies, the beloved buddy cop comedies, the dates of the best Grateful Dead live shows, the Southern Gothic short stories, the trendy boutiques in Charleston, the flattering cuts of jeans, the universe of denim, the right place to pin your bangs, the cool way to put someone down, the cartoons you were supposed to have watched each Sunday, the way to pronounce the letter "e"? Can you learn the salads and cream sauces to eat and the Crystal Light powders to drink and how much of each and when and how quietly or loudly? Can you do it convincingly?

After a week of disappearance, Mama and Baba went to the police and ordered posters that announced he was missing.

They tracked his credit card statements, which lagged behind as he drove aimlessly around Pennsylvania, drifting through motels and motor inns like a ghost. Mama didn't worry until the statements stopped completely and she began to fear what she felt was inevitable.

Baba consoled her by turning to the bagua, a Chinese method of fortune-telling, and returned with reassurance. What does it mean when the authoritarian of your family also controls the tools for telling the future? He told Mama not to worry, that the bagua predicted that Big Brother was destined either for sickness and success or good health and failure. It did not name death. Baba made a bet with Mama. (Like two children playing together.) If Big Brother was alive, she would pay Baba a dollar. If they learned he was dead, Baba would pay Mama the dollar instead. When you become habituated to tragedy, I imagine you learn to be okay, somehow. Believing in fate relieves you of some of the pain; it relieves you of the responsibility to look closer, too.

BIG BROTHER RECOVERS AT HOME and returns to college to finish a degree in English. He enters a master's program for Chinese history. Mama and Baba are so thrilled by his accomplishments that Baba gives him his Rolex to wear and buys him a Mercedes coupe convertible to drive.

When Little Seed graduates high school, Big Brother lets her borrow the Mercedes for the summer while he is traveling abroad, and she zips around to her friends' houses around North Carolina, the hot July wind whipping through her hair. Soon, she'll attend college at the University of North Carolina, but for now she enjoys the extended reverie of these precious months, attending parties and adventuring with her friends, with whom she's created home, however briefly. Soon, they'll move on to new worlds.

She is noticed all summer. The cute white boys from school tell her how nice she looks with the top down. The freckles on her cheeks are golden, and a pair of Chanel sunglasses pushes her hair back. She wears polo oxfords in pink pinstripes. She is pleased to see the efforts of her four years reflected back to her in their eyes. She feels so convincingly like everyone else now that it's impossible to name what is hers and what is theirs. She is exquisitely visible and somehow, still, not at all.

As she drifts across the highways of North Carolina, the kudzu on electricity poles and wires like a shroud, she is inundated by memories of Big Brother wandering Pennsylvania like a ghost. How frightened a person must be to run like that.

CHAPTER 14 \\\\ Filmy Ferns and Epiphytes

INVISIBILITY IS A FERN QUALITY TOO. In tropical places live filmy ferns, whose pinnules are like kelp or parchment paper. The leaf tissue is just a few cells thick and requires humid environments to stay hydrated. The pinnules don't have any mechanism for stymieing water loss, so they desiccate into onion skin. Traditionally, their family Hymenophyllaceae is divided into two genera: *Hymenophyllum* and *Trichomanes*, depending on a slight morphological difference in their sori. In most *Hymenophyllum* species, the spores are cupped by their indusia, like an oyster cradling a pearl. The sori of *Trichomanes* form tiny cups at the tips of their pinnae, which fill up with a plug of spores, like a cork. They're also known as bristle ferns because a wiry hair protrudes from each sorus.

Filmy ferns have evolved into many intricate designs. Some are simple, tiny fronds pasted to the ground like jelly stars. The kidney-shaped pinnae of the kidney fern, *Hymenophyllum nephrophyllum*, are lined by sori that look like pale tubes. The fern looks like a hat with a fringe. The Appalachian filmy fern, *Trichomanes boschianum*, which is native to the East Coast, has featherlike fronds that drip from the ceiling of caves in colonies, like emerald taffeta.

Some of the filmy ferns have developed iridescence, an adaptation that can't be captured by photographs. In person, the surfaces of iridescent ferns shimmer metallic green or deep indigo depending on where you stand, how the light filters in.

Iridescent ferns are some of the rarest species and exist only in the deepest reaches of tropical understory, where almost no light reaches. Red light, which is the most efficient for photosynthesis, is especially scarce here, having already been captured in the canopy and by taller plants. Scientists hypothesize that the unique cell walls of these ferns allow their pinnules to capture and absorb more light, and more red light in particular. This adaptation is what also makes them iridescent, a kind of pragmatism that allows them to thrive in such strenuous conditions, to grow so lushly given so little. The fantastic color is incidental, simply an artifact of survival.

IN TROPICAL PLACES, many ferns are epiphytic, meaning they grow with the aid of others. They scramble onto higher ground for sunlight, collect debris as it falls from the canopy for nourishment. Epiphytic ferns are not parasitic, but they aren't symbiotic either. Instead, epiphytic ferns perch, they assimilate, independent and indivisible from their partners. It's clear what they need, and they get it. My brain has a hard time translating this relationship—a commensalism that doesn't require harm or exchange.

I'm sorry, though. I know that even in drawing this question I'm trespassing over the boundary of observation—allowing what is inside of me to leak out into the external world, to demand answers of life that I'm not part of. But if I spill out enough times, if I ask the question of everyone and everything, won't I eventually find someone willing to answer? Someone to grow on, someone to show me the way, validate my condition, give me the answers I'm desperate to know: Am I good? Am I enough? Am I here at all? What is a need and how do you fill it? Without harming others or yourself? Without owing a sum? I look at a fern winding itself around a fallen tree branch and wonder how to even identify it without its context, without the greater body on which to mold itself, from which to hang?

A epiphytic fern that is common as a houseplant is the staghorn fern, genus *Platycerium*, named for its fertile fronds' resemblance to antlers, forking at their ends. Its sterile fronds look like lily pads, and in the wild, these basal fronds laminate to the bark of host trees, in tropical forests, to protect its rhizomes. Sometimes, the lily pads are lifted at their edges, into a basket shape, in order to collect water and falling leaf litter that decomposes and provides additional nutrients for the fern. In the case of *Platycerium ridleyi*, the fronds wrap snugly around tree branches in order to provide shelter for ants within their root ball. In exchange for safe habitat, the fern absorbs nutrients from the waste of the colony.

The spores of *Platycerium* carpet the backs of their frond tips, so the fern appears as though it's been dipped in umber paint. Staghorn ferns depend more reliably on a second method of propagation, in which their basal fronds develop in layers underneath older basal fronds, eventually collaging a surface with many overlapping moons, like a cabbage. Eventually, they fuse onto a branch or a trunk. They are not of the tree, yet they are indistinguishable from it.

ANOTHER COMMON EPIPHYTIC FERN is the bird's-nest fern, genus *Asplenium*. Its long, ribbonlike fronds unravel radially from a central point, creating a nest that perches on tree branches. Like staghorn ferns, it collects organic matter in its vases to feed on, since it isn't rooted in soil. At least one actual bird, the Madagascar serpent eagle in Hawaii, has been observed building its nests in *Asplenium nidus*, lining the basket of the fern with leaves and twigs before laying its eggs inside.

Similar in appearance are the basket ferns, *Aglaomorpha*, which develop strikingly dissimilar fertile and sterile fronds. Their fertile fronds are leafy like classic ferns, growing several feet long. Their sterile fronds, known as nest fronds, are miniatures of the fertile fronds that accumulate around the base of the fern. They remain erect even as they die and dry up, and collect thickly enough to eventually form a nest of leaves that can collect organic debris and water.

Basket ferns grow large enough to shelter their own complicated universes. Pythons are known to warm themselves in their heat when it's cold outside. And their fertile fronds produce a nectar that attracts ants, which become coated in its spores and distribute them as they wander in and out. The ants also protect the plant from other insects. The humidity created inside the basket eventually produces enough detritus that it creates a loam fertile enough for fungi and even smaller ferns.

THEN, THERE ARE THE EPIPHYTES known as footed ferns. Their rhizomes wrap around substrates and grow thick, even furry. Wrapping themselves around the midsection of a tree, the rhizomes resemble the paws of rabbits, squirrels, and kangaroos. The caterpillar fern, *Polypodium formosanum*, produces sleek silver-green rhizomes that recall larvae at the precipice of metamorphosis. The possum tail fern, or *Davallia pentaphylla*, grows thin, tapering pinkish rhizomes covered in fine black hairs.

The rabbit's-foot fern, *Davallia fejeensis*, is the most commonly cultivated species. Its elegant, slender rhizomes grow thick with golden velvet. From these feet sprout triangular fronds that resemble carrot greens. In the wild, they wrap around the trunks of trees. When cultivated in soil, they're eager to escape. As the fern matures, its rhizomes creep over the soil and wind themselves around the structure in which they are held.

Eventually, the rhizomes become so thickly knotted that the fronds lift from the pot, attempting to creep onto some other surface. I identify with the confusion of freedom and confinement, the temporary usefulness of a pot. I see myself in the searching root and wonder, again, What is a need and how do you fill it?

CHAPTER 15

THE LAST TIME THE SPIDER lived in America, he had been handsome. With a full head of hair and penetrating brown eyes, he was dreamy in that Connecticut way—lacrosse sticks and thick wool sweaters, dropping acid each weekend in a friend's basement, chasing girls with feathered blond hair. But after school, he'd left for a job in Beijing as a reporter for English papers, James Dean on a motorcycle racing through streets teeming with Chinese, picking up scoops during the country's turbulent eighties and nineties.

Now, more than twenty years later, he finds himself in North Carolina. He is beginning to stoop, the skin on his body becoming loose and translucent, the hair on his head thin enough to show glossy scalp. Like stepping out for a cigarette and coming back inside and finding that someone had swapped his body. He dons baseball caps, oversized T-shirts, and the kind of khaki cargo shorts that camp counselors wear. He makes his voice soft and unauthoritative, watches everything carefully from under the brim of his cap.

In California, he'd met a guru who was Beijingren, but tall, dark, and ageless. Like the Spider, Master Wang had also roamed Tiananmen Square during those devastating nights of bloodshed, heard bullets in the air, seen students lifelessly draped over each other's shoulders. He fled. In America, he turned to Buddhism, finding solace and healing in the constraints of mystic Chinese wisdom of food as medicine: eschew animals and the heavy protein of nuts, beans, and legumes. No drugs like caffeine or sugar or alliums or starches. Only fruits, vegetables, seeds, and earthy pu'erh, steeped continuously. Just one meal each evening: a thin stew of quinoa, squash, and greens—wild fennel if you could find it. On such advice, Master Wang had turned his mother's hair from white to black, had engineered his own eternal-seeming youth. He told the Spider: If you eat like a bird, you will fly.

IN NORTH CAROLINA, THE SPIDER is hired at Duke University to lecture on Chinese studies and to help with the student newspaper. The job mostly amounts to attending events and getting to know students of Chinese descent, students who are learning Chinese, students who are curious about China, or some combination of the three. He slouches across campus, clutching a mason jar of hot tea tucked into a sock. Sometimes he carries a ragged backpack on his shoulders, sometimes he wheels a rusted blue bicycle beside him.

He tends an unruly garden in the backyard of the shared house where he lives, scattering squash seeds across worn-out soil. His housemates are mostly graduate students, and he offers them and their friends free vegan dinner any night they want: a bowl of his humble quinoa stew. And so, on weeknights, a lively party often emerges at the picnic table in the backyard by the garden, voices cheerful and argumentative, faces golden in the fading light.

Sometimes the Spider brings out his guitar to play standards: John Prine, the Beatles, Neil Young, and they all sing together until they have had too much to drink. The Spider likes to tell the story of how, when he first went to China to teach English as a teenager, he'd play "I Am the Walrus" for his class and encourage them to analyze the lyrics. The punch line is that he had to explain to his perplexed students that it's a nonsense song, something just for fun. He punctuates this with a laugh, as if it reveals something profound about Chinese disposition, underscores the missing thing in Chinese people that he is able to provide—the goodness of absurdity, genuine Chinese laughter, forbidden Chinese joy. He is the American key in the Chinese lock.

He's so cool, the students think as their vision blurs, imagining the world his stories belong to. How old is the Spider? they wonder, tabulating it in their heads—at least the same age as their fathers, their professors. If they squint just enough, they can imagine the Spider in tweeds, in blue oxfords and baggy belted jeans, but the man in front of them has the quality of youth, in his threadbare T-shirt, an acoustic guitar over his shoulder. He tells vulgar jokes, spins stories about women and drugs and foiled plans. He rolls his eight eyes when they bring up the idea of desk jobs and graduate school. Live another way, he says.

They wonder if it is his untraditional life, doubled by China, that has made him so alive. Or if it is really the exclusion of heavy foods, a single meal a day, a dedication to reducing harm for all sentient life. Live like water, shed all earthly attachment. One by one, they clear their bowls and glasses from the table, bearing them inside, sidestepping the garden whose shooting stems and creeping sticky leaves weave in and out of one another in the summer breeze, together a fantastic new life-form, its spindly structure arcing and creaking against the brief indigo sky before darkness falls.

THE OLYMPICS WILL BE HELD in Beijing that summer. Thousands of Tibetans ask the world to pay attention to their oppression by the Chinese state. After months of peaceful protests in Lhasa, hundreds are killed or go missing. The Uighurs in Xinjiang protest for independence too, and millions of Beijing residents are evicted from their homes in winding historic *hutongs*. These homes are razed in order to make space for buildings shaped like bird's nests and soap bubbles.

These stories attract the attention of the American media. Little Seed is glued to the news. She's reminded of her home, where China is discussed and invoked constantly, like a shameful uncle she's never met. Now, everywhere she looks, there is China, again, the obsessed-over stranger: Chinese human rights violations, Chinese poison in baby formula, Chinese dissidents stripped of their basic rights. Chinese people are either ruthless or too uncivilized to know better. The Chinese will never catch up to Americans. Or China is an immediate threat, a rising power.

Big Brother is studying Chinese history for his master's degree, but his absence still lingers inside of her. Without him, she feels lost, but she's determined to find a new way for herself. When she asks Mama and Baba about China, they simply make a distinction between old China, where they are from, and new China, which started after they left. They agree with American reports that new China is gauche and greedy and individualistic. They feel sorry for the Chinese who came after the Cultural Revolution, who have lost their histories. Speaking to them about the politics of China makes her feel connected. Something about this surprises her. Big China, China as it exists in newspapers, offers a way to be close to her family without reentering the cramped China of her childhood. Or dwelling on how distant Big Brother has become.

Little Seed is becoming a journalist.

In Chapel Hill, she observes the international students in her journalism classes who are from China. She feels a faint repulsion at their seriousness. They feel foreign. Do they think of her as linked to them? She cringes. (She is not like other Chinese people.) But they naturally embody something she lacks. She wants them to recognize that she is Chinese too, but they never do. For some reason, that makes her feel angry and sententious. What of China does she contain?

She attends a lecture by a professor from Beijing on the crisis in Tibet. She is on the side of Tibet, of course. She arrives to a full auditorium, brightly lit by morning sun, attended mostly by international students from China, dressed plainly to her eye. She is wearing a gray sundress with sunflower-yellow Converses. Her hair falls in waves to her waist. She'd traced her eyes in black eyeliner. The last year of beer and cafeteria food has added an extra twenty pounds to her body, which she confronts when she sits down. The air is filled with chatter in Mandarin that she wishes she could interpret. She has been taking classes in Mandarin, but only for three semesters.

The professor, in aviators and a polo, walks to the podium and the room grows silent. He announces that he will give his remarks in Mandarin rather than English, and Little Seed feels annoyed and slightly embarrassed. But she's too close to the front of the lecture hall to leave. She tries to pick up a sentence here or there. Eventually, when it's time to ask questions, they are all in Mandarin. One voice politely and firmly disagrees with the content of the lecture. From the languid pace of the Mandarin, Little Seed recognizes words like *freedom*, and *justice*, and *heart*.

"My Mandarin is not proficient enough to speak confidently on complicated politics," the voice continues in English, soft and apologetic. "So I hope you all don't mind if I continue in English." Heads turn. The Spider is sitting in the very back of the room, wearing a knit cap, and Little Seed feels relieved to see another American here. She is impressed that his Mandarin is so good, like a real Chinese person.

The Spider goes on to speak of the brutality he witnessed and endured as a journalist in China. Little Seed is in awe. He speaks of starting an English-language magazine in Beijing, of the Chinese police breaking into his home, shooting his dog, and throwing him into a dank cell for two months before deporting him. "The Tibetan people deserve rights," he says. "The Chinese government must learn to value human life."

Little Seed approaches the Spider nervously after the lecture and introduces herself as a journalism student. She asks if she might interview him for a class assignment. He smiles and agrees, and asks her questions about her studies as they exchange phone numbers on a sheet from his reporting notebook. A real reporter's notebook! Little Seed thinks. She thanks him for speaking up at the lecture on behalf of Tibet and for agreeing to help her.

Leaving the auditorium, Little Seed feels proud for having approached someone who is so important. She leaves excited; she has uncovered something that might finally put her on a path to understand what it means to be Chinese.

LATER THAT EVENING, as she is reading in bed, a new number lights up her phone. She picks up, and before she can say hello, the Spider's voice unfurls as if in midconversation.

"The students are going wild over here on campus," he says. "Some are protesting China, and others are counterprotesting Tibet. Things are going to get ugly. You're going to want to come out here first thing tomorrow morning."

Little Seed hesitates, thinking about the plans she's made with friends to have breakfast in the morning then lounge around in bars and drink until night. She wants to know who hooked up and what everyone wore and talked about. She wants to be invited to a house party or to a football game. She wants to sit in the corner of a patio, flushed from cheap beer, and have someone notice her. She dithers.

"You want to learn about journalism, right? Well, here it is. Come along," the Spider says, irritation in his voice. "Meet me in the Duke auditorium at ten." Little Seed senses that if she doesn't go, she might lose her chance to know him.

"Okay," Little Seed says. "Okay, I'll be there." There's a pause on the other end of the line, as if the Spider hadn't expected Little Seed to say yes.

"Your people are crazy," the Spider says, gently now.

"My people?" Little Seed asks, bemused. Does he mean college students? People from Tennessee?

"The Chinese," the Spider clarifies.

"But I'm not—" Little Seed begins, but the line is dead. Yet she's filled by the feeling of being identified as Chinese, of being placed somewhere for once. Her people, she repeats to herself, a deep thrill moving inside her.

CHAPTER 16 \\\\ Fern Allies

SOME FERNS LACK the classic structures entirely: no pinnae, no fiddlehead, no sori—horsetails, for instance, of the genus *Equisetum*, resemble reeds. Whisk ferns, genus *Psilotum*, spindly coral. Because they look so different from standard ferns, Linnaeus classified them as mosses or as fern allies, distinct from true ferns. Along with mushrooms and algae, they were categorized as cryptogams because their reproductive cycles were hidden. (During World War II, the British government mistakenly hired an expert in cryptogams—the marine biologist Geoffrey Tandy—rather than cryptograms to decode German static.) Later, taxonomists reorganized the fern allies into a category alongside ferns, in their own division of the Kingdom Plantae called Pteridophyta, distinct from mosses and seed-bearing plants.

In the twentieth century, as the fossil record deepened and DNA sequencing became more advanced, the classification of fern allies broke open again. Lycophytes (which comprise club mosses, spike mosses, and quillworts) were discovered to have an ancestral lineage distinct from true ferns and seed-bearing plants. The other fern allies (horsetails, whisk ferns, and moonworts) were reclassified as true ferns because they share a common ancestor with ferns and seed plants. This new evolutionary understanding of lycophytes made the category Pteridophyta paraphyletic and therefore obsolete.

In recent years, the term *fern ally* has technically been retired, but it's still commonly used when describing weirder genera of fern. And you still find lycophytes in the field guides, despite the fact that they aren't technically ferns anymore. Precision is important, but something gets lost kicking lycophytes out of the fern world and assimilating the fern allies into true ferns. I still call all the vascular spore-bearing plants *ferns*, and I think the idea of fern allies is important for understanding. Are we meant to keep revising the present when the past imposes itself? I'm not sure it's that easy.

IN THE FIELD GUIDE of my own lineage, I'm an ally rather than a true specimen, despite having the same point of origin as the rest of my immediate family. I move my body like a Westerner; I am lukewarm on collectivism and Chinese social expectations. I am spike moss in a gully of bracken.

I see how this rearing was deliberate and generous—my parents wanted me to become American, which evoked freedom from the unending obligations of caring for elders, siblings, cousins, and in-laws; liberation from the cycles of melodrama over money and inheritances and love (both of my parents have a devastating story about becoming estranged from a sibling because they forbade that sibling from marrying someone because of their class background). It is all very Chinese, this duty to ensure a lifetime of unbroken safety and honor for one's family, even at the risk of scrambling their own sense of intimacy and connection. Everyone is always cutting each other out of their lives, leaving the ugliest voice messages on the answering machine. One's position in the family is conditional on what others believe that it should be. My family is rigid about identification with one another and with the whole. We lack the flexibility of taxonomists, to allow things to break apart and come back together.

There's another reason, too, why I am an ally to my family. Girls, in my family's culture, are considered the throwaways of the family unit because they are groomed to marry into other families. There's no return on investment. The only concern my parents ever shared with me about love was making sure I knew that it was important to choose a man with a family who would care for me at least as well as my own original family has. There were some advantages to being unseen—I was allowed to grow up wilder than my brother; the expectations my parents had for me were relatively low. So long as what I did didn't affect how well I'd be able to marry (by being a bad student or being unfeminine or having sex), I mostly escaped their gaze, as if we still lived in pre-Revolution Shanghai and not an Appalachian enclave of Tennessee.

On the other hand, American culture remained partly indecipherable, an acquired set of signs and symbols, and my family still judged me based on clearly absurd "we are like Chinese Kennedys" standards. I was pushed out into the world under the premise that relationships were transactions to be made and that I had to satisfy the family's expectations if I wanted to return home. Even if I didn't believe in this story, it frightened me that my parents did. It pushed me deeper into the world, into America, to find a different story, to escape the notion that I was just a thing to be given away. I was desperate to test the notion. I wanted to know that I could leave and still come home. I wanted to know that I could do exactly as I wished and still be wanted.

These conflicting expectations and ways of making meaning made me more than a little reckless and susceptible to pursuing safety by changing myself or forcing others to change. I was navigating an American sea by Chinese stars; the people around me were tallies of expectations, insecurities, needs, desires, and judgments that I could leverage to gain what I needed: intimacy, work, validation, whatever. I thought that was the definition of community and became an expert at knowing the names of other people and naming them myself, but it was impossible for me to actually know them this way. It never occurred to me that names are a gloss. I buried myself in names and thought I was in the world rather than on it.

IN MY FAMILY, names are mirrors and wishes. My maternal grandfather renamed my mother and her two sisters when they were teenagers, to make them appear more Western, as the culture of Shanghai became increasingly cosmopolitan. Xuying became Li Li, and when Li Li came to the United States, she became Lily. But my father, who has known her since they were both quite young, still calls her Xuying now and then, when he is exasperated, appealing as if to a child.

My great-grandfather, whom I have always known as Ta-gong, passed before I was born. In the custom of his time, he was given a private name, something that only those closest to him could use. My father was named Sheng, the character for *liberation*, because he was born in 1945, the year the war ended. But at home, he was called Sheng Nu, or "son." His sister was called Ah Nu, a tender diminutive for a daughter, and when they immigrated to West Virginia in the seventies, the locals transliterated their nicknames into Sonny and Honey. It wasn't until my father left West Virginia and became a physician that he began using his given name again.

Tagong gave my brother the name Wei Kang, a homonym for the English "Welcome," because before he was born, the family knew that my father would leave for the United States. In Chinese, the characters mean *safety* and *health*, protective wishes for a family launched across the ocean. In America, he went by the diminutive Con Con at first, then, when he was older, the more straightforward Wei. When he left for college on the GI Bill, he discarded this name again, choosing instead to be called by his middle character, Kang. That definitive, single syllable with its percussive beginning, the remaining sounds like an arcing tail. It was authoritative, like a fist on a table.

When I was born, my parents were tempted to name me Wei Lai, the characters of which sound like the words for "to come back" in Chinese, which I realize now betrays some deep longing for their original home. The first character shared with my brother, twin wishes for protection. Instead, months before he died, Tagong had given me the name Wei Xiang.

The second character in my name is associated with flight, not the upward stroke of a bird taking wing, but a relaxed downward stroke, that same bird floating in the calm, unfurling air. I was aptly named—I'm always trying to acquire safety and freedom, to gather as much of both as I can carry. For a long time, no one called me by my Chinese name. Shortly after I was born, my parents asked an American neighbor to give one in English. I hate this name now and am reluctant to mention it.

Inside of our family, we referred to one another by our place in the hierarchy, by the steps of our branching—Mama and Baba, for my mother and father. Then, my brother, whom we called Gu Gu, "older brother." Then me, Mei Mei, "younger sister," the words like a river stone or a seed, small and round in the mouth.

In our home, it was forbidden to call someone older by their given name. Your belonging was conditional on your subservience. I was smacked for calling my brother by his given name, when I was young and my curiosity outweighed my fear. I fell in line, learning to find comfort and a degree of exploration in submission. I learned to love hearing him call me by my English name when we were outside of our home, away from our parents. To wander the American territory was also to invent it, to close the space opened between us by the rigidness and violence of our home. To be named by him in that new world was to be someone else.

After I left for boarding school, I again tried to call him by his given name, thinking enough time had passed for the dumb rule to be meaningless now that we'd both left home. But when I addressed him by his given name on the phone, he became apoplectic, his speech clipped and loud. He was looming above me. He called me a disrespectful little girl and warned me against calling him by his name again. I was seventeen. He was twenty-eight.

CHAPTER 17 \\\\

THE SPIDER PICKS UP HIS PHONE and waves at Little Seed through the glass of the auditorium as she walks up the stairs to the front door. He's wearing the same clothes as the day before, gesticulating at a woman in a navy suit. He bears his mason jar in its cotton gym sock, his face shifting between seriousness and laughter. When the woman speaks, he pauses, unscrewing the lid of the jar, taking slow sips, nodding intently.

The Spider smiles and waves. He introduces Little Seed as a journalism student and the woman as a bureau chief for the *New York Times*. She's covering the protests the Spider mentioned the night before. Little Seed feels starstruck, right on the edge of a story being made.

The bureau chief has to run to an interview. She shakes one of the Spider's hands and thanks him for his advice. She searches through her purse and, turning, hands Little Seed a card.

"It was nice to meet you too," she says. "You should write to me. We're always looking for stringers in the Southeast." She smiles, and Little Seed feels light-headed, running her thumb over the print on the card over and over again as she holds it. Her life is happening so quickly. She beams and sees in her periphery that the Spider is grinning at her.

"Let's take a walk and I'll catch you up on what's happening," he says, leading her to a parking lot where a car with pop-up headlights and rusting baby-blue paint sits. There are bales of hay stacked in the back seat. Pieces of straw litter the car, and eucalyptus wafts from an electric diffuser stuck in the cigarette lighter. Paperbacks cover the floor beneath the passenger seat—*Zen and the Art of Motorcycle Maintenance*, *The Dharma Bums*.

Little Seed hesitates for a moment, noting the disrepair of the car, feeling a little uncomfortable. But wouldn't this be completely normal with any of her friends? She reflects on the incongruence of the Spider's status—his ease with prestigious journalists, his years of experience—with his casual appearance. She is drawn to his lack of awareness of being perceived. After so many years predicting the expectations of her family and the external world, she needs to be where perception and judgment are . . . unwound.

This universe, in this car, the absurd bits of straw wafting through the afternoon light, the ripped upholstery, and his ragged T-shirt and baseball cap—another Little Seed might be repulsed by the weirdness, the blurring of what is all right. But she chooses, instead, to find in it a new kind of world, a reality immune to expectation, jangling with possibility. The landscape shifts from Duke's imposing Gothic spires to the tony false brick suburbs to the dilapidated ranch homes of the countryside, tilting off their foundations, to a bottomland forest exploding with sunlight, the canopy gossamer above.

THE SPIDER SPINS STORIES as they wind their way by the river, the summer lush and damp and laden with the smell of water and mud cool in the shade. "What happened was that there was this crazy fucking protest, a handful of university students from the human rights club protesting Chinese human rights violations, which is obviously their right, but, fucking, I mean—all these Chinese students get wind of it and start calling up their buddies from across the state, Chinese nationals, and they're pissed. 'Hey, dude, they're'—fucking . . . anyway. They just mob the place. Hundreds of them. I mean, those college kids had no idea what they'd gotten themselves into. No idea."

The Spider laughs bitterly, pauses from walking, and takes a sip from his sock. Little Seed stops too. *Kuxiao bude*, he says quietly, staring at the forest floor, the tones of Mandarin ramp-like in his voice. "You know what that means, yeah?" he asks her, screwing the lid back on his jar. Little Seed shakes her head, wincing at being found out for not being . . . not Chinese enough? Not studious enough? Not worldly enough? Whatever it is, she feels exposed, wishing that there is something she might have done before this moment to have arrived at it in full flower.

"It means . . . you have to laugh to keep from crying," the Spider says, and she senses disappointment in his explanation. She repeats the four characters back to herself silently in her head as they keep walking, memorizing them. *Ku-xiao. Bu-de.*

The spruce and pine open onto a sun-bright quarry. Rainwater, pristine and glittering, has filled the open pit, lapping at sun-bleached white rocks. The light turns gold while the Spider reminisces about attending the university and spending hours in the woods, swimming in this same quarry. It is totally crazy, they agree, to think about how he'd been in Beijing for so long and has now wound up back in the same spot.

Little Seed nods along as she listens, thinking about the expanse of time, about how much can change, about how she'd like to look back one day, like the Spider, and contemplate all she could not have known. She is listening for the ways she might press herself into his mold, win his approval, grow into Little Spider. Mama and Baba always say that the right people will cultivate her so long as she is well-behaved and pleases them.

"You know, what I'm really here to do is start a new magazine," the Spider says, placing one of his feet on a flaking rock and wrapping his many arms around his many knees, gazing into the water. "I used my own money to finance the first issue and I wrote all the copy, just to prove to investors that it's a good idea," he says. "The Dalai Lama is on the cover."

"Wow, really?" Little Seed says, mimicking his posture. Minnows dart between algae, dragonflies skimming the surface, disturbing the thin sheen of light on the water.

"Oh yeah," the Spider says. "He's an old friend." He winks.

The Spider drives Little Seed home. On the ride, he gives her a copy of his magazine to look at. The Dalai Lama smiles up in his scarlet-and-marigold robe. She flips through the pages, the bylines of eight or nine different writers. The Spider laughs and explains that he made up the names to make it seem as if there was a whole staff. In reality, it was just him.

Little Seed immediately wants to work for the magazine. How perfect, she thinks, a publication about China, by someone who can translate between both worlds. But she keeps her wish to herself. She doesn't want to seem too eager, and besides, she has plenty of material to use for her assignment and she's relieved that she'll soon be deposited in her cozy dorm room with her bed and books and her cheerful roommate. She thinks about how she will tell her friends about her adventure and wonders if they'll be envious.

"What's that?" the Spider says, as if he can overhear her thoughts. He gently brakes at a stoplight. She looks at him, unsure of what he means. He reaches over the center console, where her forearm is upturned, her hand holding the magazine. He presses the pad of his index finger into a small oval scar just below her wrist.

Little Seed feels the pressure on her forearm and feels the air between them shift. She is aware of his sour, unwashed smell, of how tight the car is, the roof upholstery dangling overhead. She is unsure of what it means for him to be touching her, what this feeling is. She scans her memory for a similar sensation and intentionally selects tender moments: a friend tapping her arm because she has too much to say. Big Brother helping her climb into a tree. Baba taking her pulse when she was ill. If there had been unpleasant memories to draw from, what would she have done? Would they have outweighed the desire to work for the magazine?

"It's just a scar," she says, although the half-moon mark is in fact a mystery to her. She moves her hand away and gathers her hair in her hands, tying it into a ponytail. "I cook a lot, but I'm also pretty clumsy," she says, rolling her eyes and smiling, displacing the unsettling feeling by taking responsibility for the wound, as if that is the culprit for the interaction. Does she already sense that the Spider might react dangerously had she expressed her discomfort? She looks at the magazine in her lap and the feeling recedes and becomes, like the bale of hay in the back seat, an untidy cube.

"You should be careful!" the Spider admonishes, hitting the gas. "That reminds me, though. You should come for dinner sometime. It's always a bunch of great people. I make food for anyone who wants it—it's all organic and vegan."

Little Seed looks out onto the road, considers what it means to make this new friend, wonders whether one could even become friends with someone so much older and accomplished. She is thinking about what the Spider might give to her, what she needs. But how to know, at this age, if there is a cost? She chooses to believe that she is a fern perching on a tree to better reach the canopy. She thinks back to her college life, to the friends she's missed that day. She feels envious of them, of missing out on all the gossip and fun, all the doors that might have opened to more parties, more boys, more friends.

"You'll like it," the Spider says, more firmly this time, and Little Seed looks at him, afraid that he will read her hesitation as reticence.

"Oh, yeah, I'd love to," Little Seed says, smiling, genuinely.

CHAPTER 18 \\\\
Horsetails, Whisk Ferns, Moonworts

OF THE FERN ALLIES, horsetails, whisk ferns, moonworts, rattlesnake ferns, grape ferns, and adder's-tongues are usually grouped together. None of them resemble true ferns. Instead, they look like succulents, or flowering grasses, or reeds, or sometimes even mushrooms. Their fantastic appearances make them easy to pick out among true ferns, but their smallness and strangeness make them difficult to spot in the field.

Horsetails, genus *Equisetum*, look like miniature bamboo. In its simplest form, the plant is a hollow reed that telescopes joint by joint, the segments growing thinner toward the apex and resolving in a thimble, where spores are produced. In some species, the tip contains enough silica to scour pots, inspiring another common name of these plants: scouring rushes. In Japan, the rough horsetail, *Equisetum hyemale*, is sturdy enough when dry to sand wood and metal. Some species are more elaborate, growing whorls of green strands at each joint.

Most species of *Equisetum* grow to only a few feet, but there are two giant species found in South America and Mexico: *Equisetum giganteum*, which can grow to four inches in diameter and up to sixteen feet tall. *Equisetum myriochaetum* reaches twenty-four feet tall. Their ancestors are the *Calamites*, which thrived in the coal swamps of the Carboniferous three hundred million years ago. These ancient horsetails were treelike: up to 150 feet tall, their radial leaves sturdy wooden tubes. It's common to find glimpses of these enormous horsetails in the fossil record—an impression of joints, a trace of whorled, needlelike leaves. They died back as Earth's climate cooled and, after millions of years, were eventually compressed, along with their wetland habitat, into coal.

In 1908, Robert Spruce, a well-respected botanical explorer, reported seeing *Calamites* in a thick swamp of red mud in the Ecuadorian Amazon. He said each stem was as thick as his wrist. He said he saw a forest of them rising twenty meters high. It's unlikely that his report is true—*Calamites* haven't appeared in the fossil record for 250 million years. And he didn't collect a specimen and wasn't able to provide proof beyond his own observations.

WHISK FERNS, GENUS *PSILOTUM*, look like tiny green brooms turned upright on their handles. They don't have the symmetrical quality of true ferns. Their spindly green branches instead fork irregularly and remain mostly bare with occasional enations. When mature, these enations are ornamented by cream-colored spheres of sporangia. The branches of the whisk fern grow heavy with these orbs, as if strewn with fairy lights.

Whisk ferns were once thought to have descended from the earliest vascular plants, which evolved from algae and moss. But it was later discovered that *Psilotum* evolved more recently in the fossil record, probably around the same time as adder's-tongues, or Ophioglossaceae, whose species are remarkable for containing some of the highest chromosome counts of any organism: up to 1,260, compared with 46 in humans. Ophioglossaceae comprises genera of moonworts, rattlesnake ferns, and grape ferns. They are easily identified by their shape: a single leaf ornamenting a sporophore, where spores develop, like the spathe and spadix of a peace lily flower.

The largest of these, which resembles a true fern, is the rattlesnake fern, *Botrychium virginianum*. It grows to be about a foot tall, and its sterile frond is a triangular bipinnate frond that grows parallel to the ground. Its fertile frond extends vertically, resolving in a tightly clutched sporophore of beaded sori, which resembles the tip of a rattlesnake's tail. Grape ferns, in the subgenus *Sceptrium*, look like miniature rattlesnake ferns, their fertile fronds growing only a few inches long.

Moonworts are the most fantastic of the genus. Their sterile fronds are plush like succulents, unlike leafy rattlesnake ferns and grape ferns, and develop into elaborate shapes. The sterile frond of the common moonwort, *Botrychium lunaria*, develops ten or so pinnae shaped like palm fans, arranged symmetrically around the sterile frond like a headdress. The sporophore of the daisy leaf moonwort, *Botrychium matricariifolium*, is decorated by a profusion of orange orbs of sori, like unpopped kernels of popcorn. The least moonwort, true to its name, exhibits just a single tiny leaf as its sterile frond.

I like the common names given these ferns, as fantastic as the plants themselves: in the United States, there is upswept moonwort, *Botrychium ascendens*; peculiar moonwort, *Botrychium paradoxum*; Frenchman's Bluff moonwort, *Botrychium galli-comontanum*; pale moonwort, *Botrychium pallidum*; and Little Goblin, *Botrychium mormo*, which might be mistaken for a mushroom.

These are some of the most slow-growing fern allies, taking years to emerge aboveground. Each plant grows just a single frond at a time. They are so difficult to locate that it's often suggested that when hunting for moonworts, one should target their habitats and scan the ground for the pattern that the moonwort makes with its environment rather than the moonwort itself. It helps to let the world blur a little and become porous, to let drift your lines of sight.

CHAPTER 19

LITTLE SEED GROWS CLOSER to the Spider. She tells her family, her friends, and her professors about her new friend, hoping his celebrity and accomplishments signal something about her too. When he asks her if she is free to help him with the magazine over the summer in exchange for room and board in his shared house near campus, she is thrilled, if tentative. She has noted his strange moods, has noticed that he guilt-trips her when she's not free to spend time with him. But she chooses to think of these interactions as part of his youthfulness. They make him seem younger to her.

But her job is perfect: every day she transcribes a column that explains Chinese idioms from the English-language magazine he edited in Beijing. Her friends from school spend the summer traveling or staying at the beach with their families.

Some of them have internships with local papers too, but she knows that most of them are just running coffee and errands. None of them has the attention of a real journalist or real work to enjoy.

Every morning, they meet to take a long walk, during which the Spider monologues, holding forth on news in the world or telling stories of China, of journalism, of his former life. He expounds on the benefits of his diet, of coexisting with all sentient life. He says this is the real Buddhism, the real Chinese culture. She is rapt, remembering how slanted and mean Baba's vision of the world was. She likes the Spider's telling better. She agrees with it. He opens up to her and says the reason he'd really left for China when he was twenty-one was that his high school sweetheart passed tragically of meningitis, seemingly overnight. Devastated, he left the United States and everything he knew behind. Little Seed sees him wipe his eyes in her periphery. Then, straightening himself, he shifts his tone and begins dreaming out loud: he wants to start a new magazine. There is a place for her in it.

"Very soon," he says to Little Seed, in a way that makes Little Seed nervous, like she must hang on to every word, that she must report to these walks on time so she won't be left behind. She senses that "very soon" is a train that stops and opens its doors for just a few moments before rushing off again.

The Spider spins out details: It'll be like a magazine but really more like a club or a family, just like back in Beijing before the bust-up. Everyone was sleeping together, eating together. Little Seed is unsure whether "sleeping together" means . . . what it means. He'll cook a big meal for everyone to share each night. And there'll be a teahouse, too, that serves the public, offers free clean meals three times a day, gives information about Buddhism and Master Wang's way of life. They won't proselytize, though, no; radiating light will be enough. They'll grow and forage all of their own food. There will be yoga and an outpost in California. Can you smell the ocean salt? You know, some people out there, they just lie on the beach and soak in the sun and the air and it's enough for them. You don't need all the crap in your body—soy, corn syrup, caffeine. Get it? It's gonna be so much more than a magazine. They'll be sitting down to cups of pu'erh with the Obamas one day, for sure, that's a given. They are gonna show people what real Chinese culture is.

Is Little Seed included in this story? She is never sure but can make herself believe in it when it is just the two of them on these walks. The morning is sacred for this reason, brief bright hours when she can weave herself into the Spider's vision.

THERE ARE OTHER TENANTS in the house that summer—a Chinese graduate student who can't afford to go home for the summer, a dancer who is in town for summer workshops at the university. Little Seed makes friends with all of them. The Spider organizes trips into town for grocery shopping or the farmers market, and sometimes he talks to them about his plans the same way he talks to her about them, speaking animatedly to the graduate student in Mandarin that Little Seed can only half understand.

Hearing them chat, she feels disappointed and ashamed that she would assume that the Spider's plans were designed with her in mind. But she is also relieved when the magazine and the teahouse are validated and made real in the eyes of her new friends, who become as excited as she is.

They become a family that summer, sharing the Spider's vegan meals, watching the U.S. Open in the den, movies and poetry readings on the university green. And every evening, Little Seed is the last to linger, carrying the bowls and glass-ware to the kitchen at night to wash them because she is de-voted to this little home, and she wants the Spider to see this, to know that she is good and useful and, most of all, that she is loyal. He helps her dry the dishes and put them away, and she cherishes this moment, the feeling of special closeness.

One morning after their walk, the Spider gives her a thick manila folder of photographs and asks her to scan them in the university library. He says they are pictures from a roll of film he took during the Tiananmen Square massacre and had to be smuggled back into the United States. He says to be careful with them; they are irreplaceable.

At the scanner in the library, she pulls out the stack and sees that the images tell a clear story. There are crowds of Chinese students (her people?) rallying through the streets and squares under blue skies, holding hands beneath enormous red banners. In some images they are smiling, in some they hold peace signs in the air. Then night falls, and there is fear in the bodies in the images and stained clothes all over the streets.

In one image, officers in camouflage fatigues stand in front of a tank, holding automatic rifles. In another, a tank is on fire, and center right, a man hangs in midair. He appears to be leap-ing at the tank, his hands grasping for the flames. Then it is day again. Medics in white coats wheel bodies on carts through Tiananmen Square, then lifeless bodies under white sheets, sit-ting in pools of shared blood on the tile floor of an empty class-room. She breathes deeply as she studies the images, thinks of a young Spider behind the lens. What does it mean to have been present for this?

It is dizzying to touch history in this way, to move it across the library scanner, to look down through the photos into a

China foreign even to her parents. She is the bearer of precious evidence, of a portal to a time that has been erased. She returns the photos to their folder. Her hands are warm. She has earned the Spider's trust. In exchange, he has given her a key to the world that is also a key to herself.

WHEN THE SUMMER DRAWS TO AN END, the Spider suggests that they fly to San Francisco to interview his guru Master Wang for the magazine. She has taken up the Buddhist diet by now and has started carrying around her own jar of tea wrapped in a sock. She feels lighter, more energetic, somewhat luminous. The Spider offers to pay for Little Seed's flight to California. In exchange, Little Seed will transcribe his interview with Master Wang for publication.

It will be a good experience, he tells her, and plus, she'll be able to see how amazing the commune Master Wang has built is, where the diet comes from, and she'll get a byline out of it. But really, it's about the lifestyle. Master Wang is brilliant, he's the real deal. She'll get it, if she'll only go. And she agrees immediately, feeling as though the path she wished for on their first meeting is materializing. They'll go shortly before the first day of classes of her junior year of college. Little Seed sits on the floor in the Spider's den, watching him. He lies on the couch, laptop on his belly, buying the tickets.

The Spider closes his laptop and suggests they celebrate the end of her internship by making popcorn and watching a movie, as they had all summer with the other housemates. But their friends in the house have moved into new dormitories or gone home and the once-lively activity now feels quiet and lonesome. She sits cross-legged with her back to the couch. The Spider, who has resumed lying on the couch, extends a hand into the popcorn bowl next to her every now and again. *A Hard Day's Night* plays on the screen, and she feels lonely and begins to feel fearful about what the next year at school will hold, where she will live, if she will make new friends.

She feels an arm around her waist. She feels surprised by how light she must be that she can be lifted like a sleeping kitten. She is underneath him. Her sight becomes fragmented, and she smells skin, the odor of his body, the feeling of rough hair against her legs, hands on her body.

A cold tongue pushes into her mouth, and she thinks of her high school boyfriend, how he fumbled around her body, how they encouraged each other in their clumsiness. They would each have a pull of whiskey afterward, call on their friends to have dinner at some place with white tablecloths. It was play. She thinks about Mama refusing to have sex with Baba. She thinks of Mama telling her to marry someone at least ten years older than her. She feels an acute pain in the sudden recognition that she has been somehow formed by everything around her without actually belonging to it, and suddenly she feels as though she must make a decision, though she cannot articulate what the question is.

All she knows is that on one side of the door is her own unformed abyss, her childlike insecurity, a swirling terror of being, of what feels simultaneously like nothingness and chaos. And on the other side is just the fact of her body, a way of being defined by whatever she appears to be, what she is perceived as, what others tell her to be, a story that someone else tells about her.

She silences the frightening and inconvenient pain inside her, invisible to her family, her friends, the Spider—what is one supposed to do about it anyway—and elects to exist instead, just in this skin, in this hair, in the film between everything outside of her body and what the Spider's eyes rove over. She helps the Spider tug off her cutoffs, barely breathing, and when it is over, the Spider tells her he has been thinking about it for so long, and hasn't she? He could always tell she wanted it, and anyway, he deserves it. He deserves it, he keeps saying, he deserves it.

She observes herself pull her mouth into a smile and nod as she clumsily pulls her shorts and underwear back up. The Nantucket Reds she'd bought in high school when the Delta Blondes were wearing them. She'd made them into cutoffs when she went to college and saw they'd gone out of style. Her thighs are sticky, and she stands up, observing the dull ache between her legs, the emptiness in her stomach, the sunset streaming in through the windows. Paul McCartney's and John Lennon's tiny figures are meandering around in the TV, in black and white.

The Spider disappears for a moment and comes back with a patterned towel in neon colors wrapped around his waist just below his tattered orange T-shirt. He is giggling softly, holding a small silver box. Here, here, he is saying to her, urging her to take the box. She opens it, and rattling inside is a silver ring with a small diamond stud.

"I added up the years," he says, "and I thought it seemed crazy at first, but actually, you know, maybe it's really not." His eyes grow wet as Little Seed holds the ring up, examining it. "But she died, it would have been twenty years ago now. I always thought she might come back, you know, um, be reborn . . ." He trails off and urges her to put the ring on. When she does, he takes her hands in his.

"It's you," he says, and Little Seed is outside of herself, watching them. A couple, she thinks. Okay, she's his reincarnated dead girlfriend, she thinks. Okay, she thinks, and she takes an account of herself, just two hands, two feet, two arms, and two legs. An empty body that can nod along, can follow another body as it walks down the hallway, both bodies naked again, into a sleeping bag, on a naked mattress, in a stark white room, as a window nearby fills with darkness.

CHAPTER 20

Club Mosses, Spike Mosses, and Quillworts

LOOK, ALL I REALLY WANT is to like ferns, and truthfully I think that I do. More than tulips or birch trees or matsutake, all of which are alluring, with their own long histories and long conversations with people. I don't have to be convinced that anything else is more worthy of attention. But I think that liking is the greatest thing. It's an emotion that doesn't contain the desperation of wanting or the cost of a need, the tendency to acquire it like language or culture. When I want something or when I need it, I systematically barter pieces of myself to gain it—my belongings, my body, my heart, my mind—until it's impossible to see where I stop and the thing I have given myself over to get begins.

But when I like something, there's no picking it apart to examine its origins, no stake in what it means about me, what others will think of me because of the association. It is the rarest thing, to me, that lightness, the flutter, my imagination bursting forth, freely wandering the contours of a spindly green blade.

I'm sensitive, though, to observation. My confidence wavers when others are looking. What do I know of ferns, in front of a botanist, an explorer, a cultural historian, a book that tells me the leaves are pinnate rather than pinnatifid? With someone over my shoulder, the feeling of liking burns off. My love of ferns becomes pragmatic and mean, grows armor, deepens into a place of refuge for myself where no eyes can reach. I'm paranoid about how easy it would be for someone to take it from me with their authority, reduce ferns to the sum of specimens collected, prowess at identification, lines on a résumé.

I invent ways to defend my interest: I like ferns because they aren't in English nor in Chinese, they remind me of my own resiliency, they're everywhere. I'd do anything to keep them.

For a very long time, I hadn't yet discovered that there exists another position, neither expert nor novice, neither safe nor unsafe, free or trapped, better or worse. Nothing to be proved, nothing ever lost, nothing ever possessed. A place that is expansive and strange, that belongs only to me, so richly textured that I could spend the rest of my life studying its movements and its colors. I clambered over so many places for years without finding the threshold—my body moving through tall grass, a hand to my brow, a green flash from my periphery filling my body with recognition, of easy comfort, of something liked.

MY IMAGINATION HAS ALWAYS tumbled out of me without looking, like spike moss, trembling in a tangled thread. I have a habit of turning a scrap of interest into an entire story, into a kingdom around and inside myself. I want to believe there is something glimmering and vast under the surface. My dreamworlds are rigorous and prismatic, intoxicating to build. I've learned to become less angry when they deform against an uncompliant world. Sometimes, I can even be delighted.

The taxonomy of ferns accommodates a habit of fantasy. Plants that appear to be ferns are transformed into something nonfern by flower, by seed. Conversely, the world of ferns also invites species that don't look like ferns at all—the whisk fern, the horsetail, the adder's-tongue: gaps on the frontier. Just beyond the threshold, identification requires new ways of seeing, new categories of growth. I'm greedy about expanding the boundary of identification.

In the class Lycopodiopsida, there are three classifications of plants that were once called fern allies, but are no longer considered fern at all. Though they produce vascular tissue and spores, they are distinct because they exhibit tiny leaves called microphylls with a single spore on their surface. If ferns are a disguised plant, lycophytes are nearly invisible.

The most fernlike of Lycopodiopsida are the club mosses, genus *Lycopodium*, which look like miniature trees—they grow tiny furred branches from a wispy trunk and populate the earth like a tiny model forest, poking their way through dried leaves and pine needles. The highest tip of each tree resolves into a sporangium that resembles a miniature pine cone. They are extremely slow-growing, taking decades to creep across the forest floor like garlands. Their gametophyte forms lack chlorophyll and grow largely underground and depend on fungi for nutrients. Like tree ferns and calamites, lycopods were once giants of the Carboniferous swamps, growing more than one hundred feet high. More recently, their spores were used as microscopic units of measurement.

Another way of seeing: lycopods produce spores with so much oil that they become flammable when dried. Lycopodium powder has long been used to produce flash paper, fireworks, and pyrotechnics.

THE SPIKE MOSSES, GENUS *SELAGINELLA*, grow close to the ground. They creep, like old carpet. Their ribbony stems are lined with tiny green leaves like teeth. Their fronds grow densely packed, shingled leaves with the stiff, glossy quality of pine needles. They are known for their ability to withstand dehydration, shriveling up into brown tumbleweeds and coming alive again under the right conditions.

Unlike true ferns, *Selaginella* produces two types of spores, housed in sporangia at the bases of leaves. There are megaspores, which grow four to a sporangium and are large enough to see with the naked eye. These develop into egg-bearing gametophytes. Above the megaspores grow microspores, which are invisible and develop into sperm-bearing gametophytes.

A common spike moss on the East Coast is the meadow spike moss, *Selaginella apoda*, found in swamps and along streams. It's pale green and grows in a low pile, with threadlike stems. Its tiny leaves are pointed and slightly translucent. In contrast, another common Selaginella, dwarf spike moss, *Selaginella rupestris*, is a high pile fern. It prefers dry locations like cliffs and gravel, and grows bristles, like club moss. Its radial leaves are keeled like the hull of a boat and tighten into long spikes.

Assimilated ferns are also common: *Selaginella uncinata*, peacock fern, native to China, was originally imported as an ornamental. Its leaves branch into triangular fronds that float and turn indigo and purple. It tends to be unruly and is often

reported to escape from garden beds and nurseries and natu-
ralize to the wild.

I AM THE LEAST ATTUNED to *Isoetes*, or quillworts, the rarest and least understood of class Lycopodiopsida. They live
submerged in brackish ponds and slow-moving streams. They
produce a clutch of hollow, quill-like leaves that grow radially
around a thick, round stem called a corm, from which stubby
rhizomes dig into substrate. From the surface, they are easy
to mistake for sea grass or wild onion. Uprooted from the silt,
they recall the succulent quills of air plants.

Like spike mosses, they grow two different types of spores:
megaspores and *microspores*, which are contained within their
quills. The microspores grow within their inner leaves, and
the megaspores in their outer leaves. Tearing off an outer leaf,
one can find the sporangium—a translucent sac—in the spoon
of its base. The sac is filled with dozens to hundreds of megaspores, like a mound of caviar. Sheathed by a thin sheet of tissue called the velum, it is the largest sporangium of any plant.
Whether or not the velum covers the entire sporangium can
help identify a quillwort. But the main way one identifies quillworts is by the intricate designs of their megaspores.

Shaken into one's hand from a leaf, they dry out in the palm.
Under a hand lens, their surfaces can be geometric like honey-
comb, or puckered like the seed of a plum. Some look like the
ocean during a storm, crested with waves. Some undulate like
the folds of a brain.

Quillworts are quite common on the East Coast—the spiny-
spored quillwort, *Isoetes echinospora*, produces megaspores that
are covered in sharp spines like a porcupine. Engelmann's quill-

wort, *Isoetes engelmannii*, with quills that grow up to three feet tall, produces megaspores whose surface looks like newly mixed dough. I like their dissonance. They are the opposite of everything associated with maidenhair, spleenwort, or even club moss. There is no sprawling, no spiral, no movement except rooting. And unlike every other fern, their identification is based on the spore, its point of origin, rather than how it grows or what it becomes.

I wish my eyes would adjust all the way, so that quillworts would inhabit my recognition of ferns. I like thinking that if it were possible for quillworts to fit into my internal definition, then so much more might be possible. But how far should you push your boundaries of recognition? How fully can you abstract your understanding and your instincts before the mechanism of identification collapses?

CHAPTER 21

NORTH CAROLINA IS SWELTERING, but San Francisco sits under a big, indifferent frozen sky. Little Seed is shivering, walking through the airport as the opening ceremony of the Olympics loops on the muted televisions of the terminal. She always conflated California with summer, but the sky is porcelain and the wind, against her face, is also porcelain. The Spider wraps her in his sweatshirt as they ride in a taxi to the commune, which is attached to a teahouse in the Mission called Medicine Buddha, where Master Wang works as a healer.

On the plane, the Spider constructed like a ship in a bottle, their future together. Little Seed will transfer to Berkeley—he knows people there who can get her in. She'll study graphic design. He can tell she has a visual eye and will be able to make the magazine look good. It's a big responsibility. Meanwhile, the Spider will be the editor, will preside over the words. They'll rent a commercial space to use, he says, and she can get her yoga certification on the side and teach there.

Little Seed fantasizes about their interview with Master Wang, about the future. She imagines herself at the head of a room, lithe and graceful, urging others gently into tree pose. She imagines herself at a computer, moving columns around on a page, designing a cover. Yes, yes, yes, she thinks, feeling herself come into full color under the sweatshirt, certain this will be her one day. She imagines standing next to the Spider, reveling in a thing they have made together, a magazine with glossy pages. A home. This trip to San Francisco is just research for all of that, he tells her. She'll see, everyone there is just like them.

The face of Medicine Buddha is sherbet yellow, and there is a mural of a lavender Buddha on its face. Inside, there is an enormous table fashioned from the roots of a tree. The wood is varnished, mirrorlike. There are eddies carved into the surface of the table. A tea set perches inside one. The tiny cups glow white.

Behind the table rises an elaborate wooden screen. To the right stands a bookshelf where wheels of pu'erh tea, wrapped in thin newsprint, are displayed on plate racks. Several people sit around the table, on stools that are cut from tree trunk. They light up when they recognize the Spider and stand up to greet him. He hugs them one by one, and introduces Little Seed. She's his girlfriend, he says, and Little Seed feels a thrill. He holds Little Seed's hand and squeezes her shoulder. "Age ain't nothing but a number," he jokes, and laughs, answering the question that everyone's eyes ask. She suddenly feels engulfed by the Spider's sweatshirt, by the depths of her embarrassment, by how young she feels, by what they must look like together.

One woman with a pixie cut and a polygon face smiles at her

and says she senses that Little Seed is a water dragon, a flowing river of calm and resilience. She nods at Little Seed in approval. "Oh yeah," the Spider says, "she's on a different plane of enlightenment." He smiles at her and she smiles back, unsure of what he means, or what she has done to deserve this compliment. All she knows is that she feels glad to be good in his eyes and in the eyes of the tribe.

The Spider darts off to rummage through a refrigerator behind the tea table, and Little Seed continues chatting with the others. A large man with dirty blond hair and a square face is a tight end for the 49ers, out for the season with an ACL injury. He is staying at Medicine Buddha to recover. He tells Little Seed that Master Wang's diet and tea have helped him to heal faster than any physical therapy regimen. Another is an apprentice named José, who is training to become a healer like Master Wang. He's sweet and soft-spoken and explains to her that they all live together at this commune, with maybe another five or six people. The food is free for anyone who needs it, and everyone is free to stay for as long as they'd like.

Later, he gives Little Seed a cupping. He immediately senses by touch an old injury she had sustained years ago, a broken vertebra from a fall. He tells her about the toxins he sees in the blood raised from the cups into her skin, but tells her not to worry—in the first few months of the diet, everyone's bodies regurgitate the poisons ingested over their lifetimes. He encourages her to keep going, tells her he'll always be there to help.

"Yech!" the Spider calls out from behind them as he lobs heavy containers from the freezer into the nearby trash with rhythmic thuds. "What is all this disgusting food?" he says, holding up a container of soy-based ice cream. José blushes. "I have a sweet tooth," he explains sheepishly to Little Seed, then tries to dissuade the Spider from throwing out his food.

She watches them, feeling pity for José, for his addiction to soy-based dairy.

She has been on the diet now for nearly two months, and sticking to its rigid structures, identifying what is good food and what is dirty, makes her feel empowered and strong. Being able to categorize all of the foods so easily into those that hurt her and others and those that don't feels natural to her. She already finds the smell and taste of meat to be disgusting, and she feels nauseated when she cheats and eats foods like nuts or chocolates, in a moment of weakness. She learns to love the feeling of hunger, she feels euphoria and righteousness because she can control her hunger. She feels empathy for those who find the task to be difficult. For her, it's easy. José puts his hand on his forehead in exasperation as the Spider lectures him, face reddening, finger on the ingredients list. Little Seed watches them, pitying José, proud that the Spider rarely has to lecture her in this way.

The attention in the room shifts. A tall figure has entered, wrapped in a black *changsan*. He appears to be floating as he makes his way over to the Spider, who smiles and shoves the container of yogurt back at José. He gives the man a handshake and pulls him into a tight hug. When the man turns his attention to her, her breath grows short. He is handsome and tall, his head shaved like a monk. His face is kind and wide, and his tan skin glows. He makes his way over to Little Seed and crouches in front of her. He puts one glass in front of her and another in front of him and pours pu'erh from a teapot to the rim. Everyone is looking at them. He lifts his glass to his lips and she mimics him, her heart racing.

"Thank you for coming to see us," Master Wang says to her. "I'm from Yunnan, in Western China. But this"—he gestures to the tea table, the rack of pu'erh, the massage tables at the back of the room—"this is culture from all of China. Tea. Buddhism. Vegan diet. You should learn it and never forget." He switches to Mandarin. *We are Chinese*, Master Wang says to her, speaking softly and enunciating the tones, looking into her eyes pleadingly. *Not like them*. He winks, then stands up and walks over to José, who is fussing over the trash, where his ice cream is buried. As soon as he walks away, Little Seed longs for him to come back and pay attention to her again. She feels her arm squeezed and looks up to see the Spider smiling at her. "You're amazing," he whispers and squeezes her shoulders, kisses her on the cheek.

At night, Little Seed and the Spider squeeze into his sleeping bag, and as Little Seed drifts asleep, she watches him type an email to a friend. He is writing about her, he is calling her a wonderful woman he has just met. He is attaching a photograph of her that he found on the internet, and Little Seed feels that this description is so strange, as if the Spider's identification of her floats above her, in a language that she is not native to, and feels more real. It feels safe for the Spider to be in charge of her story.

The weekend passes in a haze of tea and chatter. She sinks into a new reality, assimilates to a group of people who genuinely accept her, who only want the best for her body and mind. She feels special to be so young, she feels special to belong to a person who is so instrumental to this community, and to Master Wang.

The Spider helps Master Wang sort through bills and edits copy for the commune's website. And though the Spider never gets around to conducting the interview he said they were there for, Little Seed forgets this disappointment easily because she knows that there must be a good reason the Spider hasn't pushed for it. She can see just how much stress Master Wang is under to pay bills and find new clients, all while providing shelter and food for anyone in the Mission who needs it. There will be a better time, she knows. They always have a home in San Francisco. What difference does a single moment of disappointment make, after all, when she has been presented with the grand and shimmering vision of her entire life?

LITTLE SEED HAS TO TELL her parents. It isn't real until she does. "Just tell them," the Spider says. "Tell them we're in love." And Little Seed feels she has to to make it real. She reflects on San Francisco, on the future, on this person who is building a life with her, and she thinks Mama and Baba will understand. She knows they will. The Spider is everything they have always told her to pursue; he is going to help her achieve the future Baba dreamed for her. He is the man that Mama asked her to find. She stands in front of the window in the Spider's bedroom as the sun is setting and calls Mama. As she explains, Mama's voice lurches from disbelief to self-flagellation.

This is my fault, she says. *I shouldn't have raised you in the countryside. I shouldn't have raised you in a place where you could never know what good men are like.* And Little Seed tells her that the Spider is a good man. She tells her again that they are in love. The sun has fully set, and the sky is blue-black, hazy with clouds.

Then we aren't going to keep sending you money, Mama says. *And you can't come home.* Little Seed thinks of home. All she can remember is anger, her brother's disappearing act. She thinks of Mama in Tennessee, alone, locked in her life with Baba. She feels sorry for her, that she never was able to experience the freedom that Little Seed knows now. She pities Mama for never having experienced real love, and the expansiveness that it provides: seeing the world for what it truly is and letting go of all attachment to it. She is made of love now, she knows, and the Spider showed her the way. *It's like I never knew food*, Little Seed says, *and now I am being fed for the first time*.

In response, Mama's voice acquires that quality Little Seed recognizes from her childhood, just before it unleashes the wordless animal wails that cannot be retrieved, and Little Seed's body buckles, searching for any human note to cling to, to try to claw back. But it's too late and Mama is screaming, *You are so stupid. You are so stupid. How can you be my daughter?* But unlike in childhood, there's an off button. She fumbles for it. At once, she is left alone with the still night and the crackle of frog song. The Spider knocks on the door and collects her. He holds her as she collapses, weeping.

BIG BROTHER CALLS LITTLE SEED, and he tells her he's coming to visit in North Carolina and make sure everything is all right. Mama and Baba are freaking out, he says. And Little Seed is full in his attention. It required a crisis, but she finally recognizes him again for who he is: the older brother who takes good care of her. She's reassured, knowing he'll come and see that she is living fully in love and smooth things over with Mama and Baba. Or, if there is something truly wrong with the Spider that she is too dumb to determine, he will know and will take her away.

The Spider and Little Seed rush around his apartment, cleaning it up and making sure it looks nice so they can impress Big Brother. When he arrives, the Spider tells Little Seed to offer Big Brother a glass of water, while he prepares quinoa soup for dinner. The Spider has put on a blue seersucker short-sleeved button-up shirt and pants and has taken off his baseball cap. He smooths his thinning hair out around his head and puts in contact lenses. Little Seed feels pleased that he would refine his appearance just for her. "Go show your brother the garden," the Spider encourages her. "Go show him how the sungolds are growing."

Little Seed and Big Brother go out to the garden. It's dusk, and they speak in English as Little Seed points out the vegetables in the garden one by one, the gumball-yellow tomatoes, the fuzzy new squash, the fat cucumbers cradled in curlicue vine. Mosquitoes circulate their legs, and they swat at them as they walk. She tells him that she is very happy, and he tells her that he's glad to see that she is happy and that she is grown up now. She feels flattered by his validation, but is unsettled to find that the words feel stilted and unspecific, as if they are scripted. She is dismayed; she feels that there is still a curtain between them. But what can she expect? She's the one who is engaged to someone more than twice her age. She scolds herself. She's lucky Big Brother came at all.

The Spider sets the coffee table, and before they begin, the Spider asks all three of them to hold hands and squeeze them, and Little Seed retreats within as she watches them chat. Big Brother and the Spider discuss Chinese history and academia. Now they are agreeing that the Chinese government is out of line. The Spider shares his experiences as a journalist in China. He is talking about Tiananmen Square, and Little Seed feels a flush of pride. She is the Spider's girlfriend. His ring is warm on her finger. And now Big Brother and the Spider are talking about her, and they are agreeing that she has a heart of gold. (A *heart of gold*, Little Seed repeats in her head, having the feeling again that everything is scripted. But whose script is this? Whose story is she in?) Big Brother looks at her, places his hand on her shoulder, and squeezes it.

"I can tell this is a very loving relationship, and that you're very happy," he says, and Little Seed chooses to indulge in the warmth of what he says rather than the strangeness of the performance. The Spider takes her hand and squeezes it too. He pecks her on the lips, and she sees that he is happy. Okay, she thinks, she's happy too.

Later, they walk Big Brother out to his car, and Little Seed hugs Big Brother and thanks him for coming. "Awww, see? Family healing," the Spider says, and Little Seed looks at him, blushing, and playfully tells him to stop. He laughs. "See? She tells me to stop!" he says to Big Brother, to prove that Little Seed is an equal partner. For a moment, Little Seed feels this way. She makes up a story that they are all just strangers who just happened to meet at the same place on separate journeys, and feels peaceful.

Big Brother puts his hands on Little Seed's shoulders and looks her in the eyes. "You call me Kang now," he says. "Okay, Big Brother," she responds, then pauses. "Kang," she says slowly. It feels foreign in her mouth. For a moment she reflects on all the times in her past when she said the name without permission and was punished for it, by him and by her parents. She remembers when he chose to rename himself, and she feels grief for his old name, the one that belonged to the brother who was her protector, her best friend, her guide. What life does he want to inhabit with this new name? Or perhaps, what is he leaving behind?

Big Brother gets into his Mercedes convertible and pulls away. The Spider wraps his arms around Little Seed's waist from behind. As Little Seed waves and watches the car grow smaller on the road, she longs to be there with him, sharing that small space with the highway stretched in front of them, listening to the radio. Terror grips her as Kang turns and the

Mercedes disappears from view, and she understands that she has made a decision.

"THERE'S ALWAYS A DOMINANT PARTNER and a submissive partner," the Spider says. Little Seed is so mature for her age. She's twenty and certainly old enough to make her own decisions. It is the dead of winter, or it is early spring, or it is a cool day in autumn. Her mother never stops sending money, and the Spider tells Little Seed that if she lets an apartment for them, he'll put his half of the rent into a savings account that will go toward the down payment on their teahouse in California one day. The grass around the new studio apartment that Little Seed has rented near campus is always faded and dry. It could be summer. The little apartment is just a room, with a television and a bed squeezed into the back, a dining table and a sofa near the front French windows and a hall with a tiny kitchen just off to the side.

Here is how you block your father's number on your cell phone, here is how you set up filters so that his emails don't show up in your inbox. "Then you can just go in and delete them all at once. See?" The Spider feels that he is in a psychic battle with her father for her soul. "Your dad's fucking insane." Little Seed loses track of time. She seems to sleep all day. The days blur into the nights. The Spider has taken her car keys. "Your car is safer," he says, and besides, he can drive you to school and pick you up every day so that you don't have to worry about parking. He brings you food when he picks you up, packed into a lunch box. Isn't this nice?

She has terrible cravings for things like peanuts and Pop-Tarts and binges on them from the vending machine during her seminars in the mornings. She asks her classmates to smell her breath, fearful that the Spider will know. She goes for a drink with a classmate, and when she comes home, he smells the beer on her breath. "You've been eating bad food," he says, his face drawn. "If you want to be young, you can go be young," he shouts. You're free, he is saying to her. "Go have fun, don't take things so serious. You are free! You're free. If you want to be." He storms away from the apartment, she hears the car speed away, and she is left at the dining room table, weeping, begging for him to come home, weeping until he does, and she apologizes over and over again and tells him she loves him, that this is the life she wants.

In the middle of the night, the Spider wakes up and turns on the light and begins to type on his laptop. He is translating articles from Chinese for important newspapers, he says. He says he needs the apartment to stay peaceful and clean so that he can do his work. If it isn't calm, he develops migraines that make him feel like his head is splitting open. He shows her how to sweep the floors, tells her how often she should sweep, how she should clean the toilet and the shower. Sometimes there is a film of brown dust on the mirror, and when she is cleaning, she finds a bottle of Rogaine behind the toilet paper below the sink. She puts it back carefully, and she wipes down the mirror and never mentions it to him, though sometimes she hears him slip into the bathroom. She hears the locking of the door, the shaking of a paint can, the sound of aerosol.

"Here is my wallet," he says. They are parked in front of Whole Foods. She has asked him why she is always paying for the groceries, why he doesn't split the bill with her. He shoves the leather wallet into her hands. "Use it," he says, his eyes daring her. He turns away from her, his hands on the wheel. "But when it's gone," he says, "that's it." She gives it back and they walk in and a cashier asks him to leave because he isn't wearing shoes. He tells them this is a free country, that he wants to speak to the manager. He is yelling about abuse but finally he leaves. Occasionally, he steals bottles of juice or liquid aminos, diverting them into the pockets of his cargo shorts.

Has it been months? Has it been years? Painful sores develop in Little Seed's mouth, and she shows the Spider. He tells her it's the toxins coming out of her. She says it's been too long. How much longer until they are all gone? She loses her period. She is fatigued and now barely sleeps.

She misses her family and is sorry she has lost them, but she cannot imagine how to make up for what she has done. Even the wrenching noise of Mama and Baba's home seems appealing now. Time moves in and out of joint, and she feels captured, as if under a jar that keeps shrinking. She can look out, but she can never leave.

On a run behind the apartment, in the woods, she hops over a small creek and comes face-to-face with a white buck with enormous velvet antlers. The deer holds her gaze. Little Seed feels frozen. The buck turns and disappears into the undergrowth. Little Seed walks home. She tells the Spider she has to see her family, and she is surprised when he allows it without a fight.

When she is home, Baba tells her he's planned an entire course to teach her the Mahayana text, the Heart Sutra, an artifact of *real China* and of *real Buddhism*. Her liquid drift congeals into blocks: one lesson in the morning, one at night. In the study where Baba once told her stories when she was a child, he gives her a laminated pink edition of the sutra and its 260 characters. They are in traditional Chinese, which Little Seed cannot read, but Baba sounds them out to her and teaches her to say them, correcting her tones gently, and expounds for hours on the significance of each character. He tells her a story of China that feels scholarly and real, less vague than the China offered by the Spider.

He coaches her to memorize the sutra line by line. *Little Seed, you already have a Buddha's mind*, he tells her. He tells her stories of his childhood to explain the various attachments expressed by the sutra. He tells her he used to hate eggplant because it reminded him of snakes. But he learned to recognize that that was just a story, just an attachment. Now eggplant is one of his favorite vegetables. He tells her that when he immigrated to the United States, he would sit on the subway in New York City, reciting the lines of the Heart Sutra to calm himself, to make all the terrible things he'd ever seen and experienced quiet down.

But the attention she gets from Baba, as nice as it feels, recalls the dangers of her childhood. Will he denounce her if she stops paying attention? If she leaves the Spider, will she have to return to this home, to Baba's story? She is trapped, knowing that whatever her life is with the Spider, it is created from similar shaky transactions of care and violence. But she has no capacity to consider the transactions she is making. Right now, she needs protection and a new story.

At the end of the week, Little Seed can recite the sutra by heart. Mama and Baba listen to her and smile and clap for her like she is a well-behaved child. She knows that she hasn't found any glimmering truth from what she has learned, but perhaps that part comes with time. In any case, the attention and the care that Mama and Baba have shown her fill a part of her that she didn't know was empty. She possesses something powerful, more *Chinese*, to defend herself against the Spider now. She drives home to the Spider and notices that the things in the studio apartment are duller, less attractive. The Spider looks at the way she looks around at the studio, at him. "They really did a number on you, huh?" he says, walking outside and leaving her alone in the newly dingy apartment.

IT IS MONTHS LATER, maybe half a year, under the pretense of nightmares and insomnia, that she seeks out therapy. The Spider tells her he should go with her, and she lies to him: the therapist says that isn't typical care. The therapist asks her to draw sketches of their apartment and tries to explain to her that she needs to find the boundaries of her own life, needs to learn to say no. Little Seed learns to disagree with the Spider; she buys yogurt at the store for herself, eats dairy and beans and nuts without guilt. She feels her body again, the contours of her own mind, her own desires.

One day she asks him for her car keys back and offers her engagement ring to him in a box, as a transaction. She makes up a story in which she is the villain so he won't be humiliated and scream at her: she doesn't want to wear it until she deserves it again. She half believes in this lie, and wonders if slipping out of the dream she has lived in for the last year is a mistake. She wonders if she will eventually beg to be let back in, to wear the ring again.

He storms out of the apartment, only coming back in the middle of the night to sit cross-legged on the bed next to where she sleeps, rocking himself back and forth and telling her she is too fucked up now, that everyone will find out she has been in a relationship with someone so much older and no one will love her, that she's crazy. She's completely fucked up and so is her family. Who will ever want her? And Little Seed believes him but also believes that even if this is the truth, it would be better to be fucked up and alone than how she feels with him. He leaves the apartment again, and she throws her belongings, a bag of clothes and some books, into her Toyota and drives away. She asks to stay with a friend from high school. Her friend asks no questions, lets Little Seed share her bed for as long as she needs, and Little Seed feels hope.

She returns to Tennessee. In the July sun, she takes a walk with Baba and tells him she's left the Spider. She unrolls an explanation, an apology: she's dishonored him and Mama, she's—he waves his hand and tells her there's no need. They keep walking, and she understands that he is teaching her how to bear torment, how to bear the unspeakable things that can live inside a person. She glances at him, sees there the Cultural Revolution. She wipes her eyes and they keep walking, and she knows that this is all either of them can do.

But she doesn't know any other world or any other way of being. She remembers Big Brother's discarded name, the character they share. She tries it on tentatively, testing its ability to carry her, like an epiphyte. When she finishes school and leaves for New York, she slips it around her shoulders like a traveling cloak. It fits. She is surprised at how simple it is to say this is her name, and to hear herself called by it. She begins to believe she can be known as something different than what she has been called her entire life. To be called a name she was punished once for even saying. *Wei*. Her mouth opens around the word, the vowel floating upward. Like a yes, like a question, like a hello.

III. IDENTIFICATION

quillwort

CHAPTER 22 \\\\ Field Guides

KNOWING THE NAMES OF FERNS is one thing; identifying them is another. I'm no field identification expert, but I have a growing collection of field guides and spend a lot of time with the ones I don't have at libraries and beat-up bookstores. Field guides almost always have two halves: first a general overview of ferns and their habitats, then a section on biology and no-menclature. I'm always delighted to find that the tone of each section can be a bit imperious, even wounded—fern people are eager to justify the study of ferns, despite and because of their subtleties, and to chide the general public for not paying better attention to this near-invisible creature of nature.

Pretty much all guides have a key that's organized like a choose-your-own-adventure story. The first page of the key offers a first cut, the highest-level cleavage you can identify—

it might ask you to decide whether the leaves you're looking at are feathery and grand or small and heart-shaped. If feathery and grand, the guide may direct you to page 66, where it asks you whether a rachis is covered in white or silver fur or bare; to page 110, whether the edges of pinnules are saw-edged or smooth; back to page 45, whether the spore's indusia are attached or unattached; and at last to the distant environs of page 201, on whether you're standing somewhere rocky and arid or humid and lush. By deciding these details, you climb down the categories of family, genus, and species. Your goal is to arrive at the right page with the right botanical drawing. Here's your fern. These are its habits, its ecology, and its growth range, its affinity for sunlight and shade.

I find forests daunting in their limitlessness, in their lush, dark complexity. But field guides make a comprehensible story of the woods, build a complex but orderly system of organization. Better yet, the creation of each guide is deeply personal, invariably involving many weird choices, making each edition its own maze. There are limitations, of course—the taxonomy and biology change but slowly, the ferns slower still, speciating across eons—but beyond that, every author is free to group the categories of identifiable features however makes the most sense to them. I like the attempts to convey order, the hope of revealing what is in a person's brain. I like learning about what is otherwise an impossibly big universe by pinging around inside someone else's rules.

I find freedom in constraint, in acknowledging how I am held so that I can move through a place without having to apply too much thought. And while the holding is usually unconscious and unseeable, sometimes, you get to choose it yourself. Today I'm carrying *Peterson Guide to Ferns of Northeastern and Central North America*, second edition. It's heavier in the hand than it looks, kelly green, compact enough to slip into my coat pocket.

BUT IN NEW YORK IN 2015, I had no woods and no ferns. I started to feel lopsided by how much I knew in theory and how little I knew in practice. I was confident in my understanding of how ferns worked and what they were called, but I still couldn't tell the difference between what was fern and what wasn't. Every abandoned lot and sidewalk crack presented problems I couldn't solve.

In the hot, windless July of that year, I had been offered an opportunity to spend two weeks writing in Austerlitz, in a little town in upstate New York, near the Massachusetts border, on the property of Edna St. Vincent Millay, a poet I'd never heard of. I was reluctant to leave my little apartment and my office job, but it was late summer and I knew it would be green. I was confident that meeting the ferns would be easy—how could it not, with how much I had learned?—so I packed up my laptop and my *Peterson* guide and got on Metro-North.

CHAPTER 23

LITTLE SEED ARRIVES IN NEW YORK prepared to invent her way forward. Donning her new name, she attempts to empty herself of her past—the pain of her childhood home, Big Brother's disappearance, the Spider. She casts around, again, for home, a container lapped at by the ocean, desperate to be filled. Everything captivates: glamorous new friends, the deep maroon of dive bars after midnight, how everyone she meets is hungry for attention and recognition and love. Has she ever belonged somewhere so much? She is relieved when she finds that no one in the city seems particularly curious about her past. Soon enough, she feels herself grow less curious about it too.

It is easy to forget, also, that her new name isn't new. It's Big Brother's old name, and to her it identifies everything she cherished about him before he closed himself off: his adventurousness, his courage, his protection of her. So, the name (her name) also represents her cavernous loss, and her hope that it be temporary. And she is binding herself to him with the name. She is so certain, still, that he will come back to her one day, if she can wait and perhaps change herself in the right ways. For now, the name is an ikon. She has named herself after what she is waiting for.

Big Brother has been accepted into Cambridge University for a doctoral program in China studies. Mama and Baba are incandescent with pride, an immense shroud lifted at last. He's found his path. Little Seed hopes that his achievement will return her the Big Brother she knew. All of them believe that Cambridge will change not only Big Brother, but the family too. And why wouldn't it? Little Seed has already noticed that his acceptance into Cambridge changes her, in the eyes of new friends and acquaintances in New York City. There is a tiny bloom of interest when she tells people that her brother is getting a PhD at Cambridge. She loves to feel transformed, in their eyes, from a provincial fob into someone with pedigree.

She begins to desire her own prestigious institution. In New York, there are plenty of people who help her strategize: cultivate the right friends, gather the right clothes, find the right parties, become worthy. Her past desire to know the Delta Blondes feels as antiquated as a tube top; the person she is becoming thinks of those girls as conventional and stupid. In the spring, an editor at a prestigious magazine hires her to be her assistant, and Little Seed begins to molt into the great new thing she is becoming.

Little Seed hasn't read the magazine at which she's hired to work. She knows that reading it is a kind of currency. She winces when she remembers how often the Spider would brag about knowing its editors and writers. How much of what she knows about American culture has his sour smell? But she's never opened an issue. What if she wasn't sophisticated enough to parse it? What if it raised a boundary between herself and the person she wanted to be?

But her senior year of college, she would sometimes walk around campus with an issue swiped from the library, feeling that the cover was transforming her, in the eyes of others, from foreign to native, from not knowing to knowing, from being the girl who had spent two years trapped with the Spider to someone un-fucked-up.

MAMA AND BABA, experts at camouflage, give Little Seed money to buy clothes for her new job. Little Seed imagines herself in a wrap dress—maybe emerald, maybe navy blue—hair slicked back into a ponytail, red lipstick applied precisely. But in the fitting room, nothing she picks out works. The pants are too long, the skirts swallow her. Just a few days ago, she had been soaring when she told Mama and Baba about her new job. She'd hoped they would be thrilled, as with Big Brother's acceptance to Cambridge. Instead, they spoke to her as if she had adopted a fragile plant that they didn't believe she could take care of.

Be the first to arrive in the office and the last to leave. Everyone will know you're hardworking. Don't miss opportunities, Mama said. Baba wrangled the phone from Mama. *Always smile and be cheerful and quiet*, he counseled gruffly. *Baba knows how American offices work. It is always the foolish colleagues who spend time at bars after work who don't advance*. If Little Seed can show that she is useful, he said, the editor who hired her might establish her career. Little Seed folds into herself again, wondering if her future will always rest in the hands of others.

Mama and Baba can't help you navigate New York City and the world of journalism, Baba continued. *But now you have someone who can show you the way, if you are good enough.*

Lately, Little Seed resents falling like a domino at any hint of paternalistic, knowing affect. She is starting to notice how quickly she gets stretched, like canvas over a frame, by the perspective of everyone else—Mama, Baba, her blond roommate, the Spider's—despite her new New York life. She is dying to embody Wei, New York, freedom. Or, at the very least, Slightly Bigger Seed.

She finds she is able to believe in her shaky reinvention when she is drinking. After seven or eight gin and tonics, her vision gets blurry and so does the external world. Finally, the center is still, and Little Seed is gone. Call me Medium Seed, boys. Or, after ten drinks, it's Big Seed, baby! She's screaming this at someone across a table, the cigarette in her hand threatening the bar's drapes. The amber Edison bulbs above the sticky bar make everyone beautiful. He is believing whatever she tells him about herself, however she is choosing to be. She's the kind of woman who drinks whiskey neat. She listens to jazz. She orders sambuca for strangers, cuts up lines in the bathroom with her Wells Fargo debit card. Pulling his face into hers, pulling him into her bed. The physicality, the connection, the danger—none of that is on her mind. She wants to be Wei for a little while.

A few hours later, in the bluish morning light, head pounding and throat doing horrible things, she wakes up as Little Seed. She's returned miserably to her container, she's apologizing to her roommate about the chaos, trying to find something to wear that will make everyone like her and leave her alone.

Anyway, back in the fitting room, she's full Little Seed. A white poplin shirt puckers around her belly and puffs out like a deflated balloon at her chest. She tries turning to the side, sucking in her stomach and pulling on the shirttails. She rotates, looking for a single good side. She feels humiliated, running her hands down the waist of the shirt, feeling her warm skin through the fabric.

Well: she can lose weight, she thinks, feeling better already. She can stop drinking for a little while, eat sparingly, if it matters for the future. The Spider enters her mind; she pushes him away, but lately she thinks of him all the time, terrified that if her editor finds out about the relationship, she'll rescind the job. Hunger is an idea she can turn off if she needs to. She replaces the shirt on a hanger. One day she'll come back, and it will fit perfectly.

ON HER FIRST DAY OF WORK, Little Seed wears a formless red shift and a pair of Acne bullet boots. She's gotten up before the sun that morning, like she used to at boarding school. She's blown out her hair and applied makeup. She's packed a notebook into a blue leather briefcase that Mama and Baba overnighted to her after finding out that she didn't own anything smart. *What would people think of her at her new job if she didn't carry a nice briefcase?* they said. They'd saved it for a long time, as a gift for someone important. She feels resentful at their advice, but can't help but feel special that that person had turned out to be her.

She swipes herself into the double glass doors of the office and crosses the lobby, her head lifted a little. It's too early for anyone else to have arrived, and she finds her cubicle in a darkened maze of felt and glass. She drinks in the sight of books on every surface, enormous posters of past covers on the wall, precarious stacks of manuscripts on desks. She imagines a future day when it will feel familiar, when she'll wander into someone's office and unthinkingly rest her elbow on a pile of famous writing. That's when she'll know that she has officially become Medium Seed.

She unpacks her bag and thinks about Big Brother. Now they both belong to institutions that deliver pieces of the future Baba had imagined for them. She feels proud that she's followed the death march to pedigree. She feels that he has cleared the path before her. It's inevitable, she thinks, that they will meet again soon.

"Welcome!" a bright voice chirps behind her. Little Seed turns and smiles at the editor who is her new boss. "Come on in," she says warmly, winking and waving her hand. Little Seed scrambles to her feet and follows her into her office, a clean, bright room filled with books. The pale daytime neon and blare of Times Square traffic forty stories below.

The editor pulls thick files from her handbag and flips through them, rearranging papers on her desk and scratching items off a notepad with a pencil. Little Seed observes quietly, noticing her tailored navy blazer and cream lavallière blouse, her hair a gleaming highlighted bronze. As she sorts, she talks to Little Seed about the world of the magazine and its organization, all the different departments and how they fit together. Little Seed consumes it like fuel and glows in the cantilevered office chair. She thinks of the stupidity of Spider's fake magazine.

"It truly is a family," the editor says. Moreover, because the editor didn't get involved with copy, Little Seed would also be spared. In fact, it would be better if Little Seed didn't aspire to write or edit. But unlike the other assistants, she would get a bird's-eye view of operations at the magazine, an intimate understanding of how every department functioned, each editor's temperament, the quirks of the writers and their agents. Little Seed would learn how the editor made it all run.

The most important thing for Little Seed to know about the job, the editor says, when she looks up, is that the filing cabinets are always to be locked, and the key carefully secreted away. Little Seed only now notices the wall of beige metal cubes behind her. In them, the editor keeps files about every writer and staff member who has ever worked at the magazine—records of how much money they make each year; records of office spats, lawsuits; revisions of complicated stories; notes on bad behavior and complaints. But also, instances of awards won and happy news—babies, weddings, promotions awarded. Vivian Gornick? File. Vladimir Nabokov? File. Hannah Arendt? Third drawer on your left. Little Seed will help the editor organize the files and keep them safe from others. Imagine the havoc if everyone had access to the magazine's vast interiority.

"It's for that reason that only one of us should ever be gone at a time," the editor tells Little Seed, looking her sternly in the eyes as she reiterates: the filing cabinets, the key in the lock, the office door lock. The structures closing in on one another and forbidden from anyone but the two of them, here in the nucleus. Little Seed's job will be to remain at her desk: she, too, is a lock and key, another coil of the tidy center that binds the magazine together. Little Seed fears that she won't be up to the task.

"Don't worry," the editor says, placing a hand on her shoulder and smiling warmly. "You'll pick it up really quickly."

SURROUNDING HER CUBICLE is Editors' Row, a gray clutch of offices and cubicles from which clicking keys and muffled conversations can always be heard. These are the editors who work on the stories that appear within the magazine; Little Seed's editor is concerned with the contracts and business that feed the magazine. Little Seed watches them drop in on one another, chat and complain about stories and writers. She often has to interrupt them to deliver her editor's messages or to remind them of appointments they are expected to make with her. Little Seed learns that her editor is loved and feared, and Little Seed bears something of this status, like a herald. The editors are attentive when she knocks on their doors, but they have no reason to let her into their world.

Little Seed spends her days filing and rearranging the editor's calendar. Around her, the assistants of Editors' Row move in tiny flocks, alighting on one another's cubicles to trade gossip and drafts. Little Seed wants to know them, but they don't seem interested in being known. In the elevator, overhearing them discussing stories, Little Seed turns a critical gaze on herself, wonders what it is about her that is too provincial, too unappealing, or too boring to belong. The assistants wear glasses and unstylish office clothing and have mussed hair, and Little Seed begins to feel embarrassed at how attentive she is to her outfits and makeup. The more insecure she grows, the more intensely she plans what she wears and how she styles herself, which only serves to make her feel even more alienated from the other assistants. But it's impossible to disarm. The language of clothing she acquired, dressing defensively for the Delta Blondes, has reëmerged in her.

Eventually, Little Seed comes to feel that her identification as an assistant is only nominal. While she still longs to belong to the little cabal of assistants, watching as they embark for lunch together, she finds herself drawn, in a way she can scarcely explain, deeper into the heart of the magazine. She adopts the inner-sanctum posture, for example, folding her arms under her chest as she walks, staring at the ground, looking up briefly with a curt smile if someone happens to greet her in the narrow hallways. Her cubicle, her editor's office come to feel like an inner chamber of the magazine's heart. There, among the filing cabinets, the calendar, the perfectly segmented days, Little Seed finds her place.

After her editor has left, Little Seed roosts in her office, straightening up and perusing the personal correspondence, expense reports, and party invitations of famous writers. Here are copies of Joan Didion's passport photos, along with a handwritten note, thanking Little Seed's editor for her help with a difficult visa application. There's Haruki Murakami's diner expenses from the Red Flame (two cheeseburgers, a chocolate malt, extra ketchup). She comes across Robert Caro's painstakingly handwritten notes on yellow typewritten pages and sees, with a tiny, static pinch of recognition, the ghost-white spine of *The Power Broker* on the bookshelf behind Baba's desk. When she comes across a writer the Spider gave her, she feels a small, unpleasant vibration and moves on.

Even more intriguing to her are the folders for the writers whose work wasn't good enough to make it into the magazine. There are folders for teachers with whom Little Seed has studied writing, files complete with the editors' critiques of their work. She feels at once smug and surprised, realizing that she has snuck into a place her teachers couldn't reach. But isn't she just a stowaway, and still outside true Editors' Row? Nevertheless, the magazine is beyond reproach, all the writers in the world its little hostages, and Little Seed sits now at its heart.

Her English is a bricolage: Appalachian vowels, the pretentious vocabulary of precocious college students ("bricolage"), the little-China English of her home, the slang and uptalk of tentative young women. It contains, like shell fragments in concrete, everything that has made her. And she is eager to trade it for the élite, overcoördinated English of the magazine, to belong, finally, to this place of greater safety.

ONE DAY, THE EDITOR OF the famous fashion magazine downstairs calls to schedule lunch with Little Seed's editor. Little Seed jots her information down in disbelief. "Totally," she tells her, in awe. "Just one second." She taps a button and waits to hear the editor pick up before hanging up. Little Seed smiles, excited already to relay the encounter to her friends. She hears the editor say her name and looks up, surprised that the call has ended so quickly.

"It seems as though we have a little hiccup," she says, smiling inscrutably. "The word *totally*. You used it on the phone?" she asks, and Little Seed nods, resisting the urge to say the same word again. The editor sighs. "The editor you just spoke with is complaining that you weren't speaking formally enough with her," she says, still smiling, rolling her eyes a little. "She asked me what kind of Valley Girl I'd hired to be my assistant." The words conjure images of blond women in bikinis and sunglasses carrying enormous shopping bags. Is this what her voice projects, she wonders? And what is the problem, if so? Little Seed flushes red and looks down at the dress she is wearing, she looks at her hands, she looks at the computer screen, where, seconds ago, she'd been adeptly rearranging appointments for the editor.

"It's okay, but just be more mindful of how you're speaking on the phone," the editor says. Little Seed nods, searching her vocabulary for words that need to be excised. This world is still conditional, she realizes. She is lucky to have been given a part, but she can't become lazy. Before she enters her office, the editor turns back to look at Little Seed. She's smiling, her hand on the door.

"Please, Madame, let us speak more formally with one an-other," she says, in a singsong cadence, waving her hands as if she is conducting a symphony, as if Little Seed is meant to sing along. Little Seed forces a smile.

CHAPTER 24 \\\\ Austerlitz

IN AUSTERLITZ, IT WAS PERFECT AUTUMN, and I stayed in a white barn with a gambrel roof that rolled over either side like heavy curtains, falling nearly to the ground. The double paddock doors on the front were expertly detailed in black paint, their crisscrossed beams stark and precise. A string of clerestory windows along the side wall, just under the roof's edge, became a precise line of golden thumbprints in late afternoon.

I slept in a small hutch by the front door, and I had a studio to write in on the second floor. For the first few days, I lay reading for long hours on a sagging leather couch in the corner of the studio in dim lamplight and intermittently imagined the process by which the barn, which had been ordered from a Sears Roebuck catalog in 1928, made its way to Austerlitz. The rise of industry had made it possible to standardize unwieldy projects, and Sears advertised that its "Modern Barn" was designed with the same advanced engineering involved in raising city skyscrapers. The kit comprised lumber cut to fit, factory-produced doors and windows, the exact number of nails and shingles required, and just the right amount of paint for two generous coats, no wasted materials—I loved thinking about the aging catalog barn that held me on the edge of a town so small it was lucky to have a post office.

The barn would have traveled in pieces by train to a nearby train depot, where it would have then been carried by horse and buggy to Austerlitz. Then, it would have been constructed on-site with half the labor a barn of its size normally required. And in half the time: 433 hours, according to the advertisement. My mind played a reel of carpenters in cream coveralls hammering in time as the sun and moon passed over the changing sky, the barn unfolding level by level, like origami. I felt unsettled by my imagination's cartoonish precision, the childlike weirdness.

The completed barn could have held horses and pigs, maybe goats to trim the clearing outside. Later, it was renovated: four bedrooms on the ground floor and a kitchenette, a small library, and four studios on the second. The staircase to the upstairs studios was unfinished, the hallway shaggy plywood, all bare bulbs and splinters. In my studio, there was a shaky wooden ladder in one corner that reached into the rafters, where I would be enveloped by a gauze of varnish and wood dust in sunlight creeping from beam to beam among junk food wrappers and mostly dead bottles of whiskey. Something about the barn attic allowed me to feel liminal, halfway in and halfway out of the stories I'd written, part Wei and part Little Seed and part autumn sunlight.

I WOKE UP EVERY MORNING wanting to hike. I'd spend hours on different trails, meandering through the woods in the autumn chill with no object, tacking upward clearing by clearing, until I lost my breath and became the quick, hard pulse of blood under my wrist.

In the woods around Austerlitz, I started to conceive of my body differently. This new conception was based on how it felt to be inside my body. Hard to believe now, but it hadn't previously occurred to me to locate the shape of myself from the inside. I felt the texture of pebbles or soft earth underfoot, for the way my legs would burn, then rest, then burn. When the grade was steep, I learned to walk tall and transmit force through the column of my body. My throat always stung in the first half hour. But then, eventually, I'd warm up and chase my thoughts and feelings in rhythm with the trail, walking outside and walking inside. I loved returning to the barn sweaty and high off some magnificent idea or question I'd extracted from the woods.

I was so overwhelmed by the experience of being in the woods I didn't see any ferns at first. Nature was its own cosmos: I was pummeled by this realization. It will always be wildly and ecstatically indifferent to my insistence on plucking out a single organism and memorizing its every facet. The green of summer slipping into ocher, the tangle of loam and brush underfoot, tiny insects weaving their way around sprays of flowers hanging from tree branches. There was no way to make a story. It wasn't about that.

But eventually, they found me. True ferns by the trail or further in—I'd carefully pick my way through, examine one, find another nearby. They taught me their patterns and habitats. Soon I was able to notice them even in my periphery. Eventually, I began collecting fronds. In my writing studio, I laid them on the long table beneath a large window that stamped a rectangle of hard light onto the chipped oak planks of the floor.

The past came to visit. That white rectangle of light belonged also to the Spider's cottage, to so many frightened months in North Carolina. I was still humiliated, still terrified people would find out, still calculated the ways and odds he might find me. For years, he would send me threatening emails, call me again and again. A decade later, barefoot in that little room on the second floor of the barn in Austerlitz, I felt relief that he couldn't follow me.

I folded in against myself, reshaping the story of what had happened into so many clean shapes, into boxes that I could shift around painlessly in my mind. I had been a brave young woman to have charged into such a dangerous experience; I was good for choosing adventure when it was presented to me; even if he had been terrifying and abusive, he had still chosen me because I was special. But the Spider still loomed in my mind. My mind would play a reel of him buying a gun, driving angrily through the night, pulling into my parents' driveway. (Funny what your deepest fear is, in the end.)

It would take more time, more than a decade, to confront that fear and that pain. I had to become safe enough on my own first. Then I was able to examine fully the terror within me and see that it was a story, like all terror, and that I had agreed to exist inside it, hoping that it would keep me safe. But when I let go of the story and came to understand that I hadn't been brave or special but that I had been stuck in a web intentionally spun to catch me, I didn't feel relieved or free. Instead, I felt the horror of a gaping hole within me, seeing—newly storyless—that my desires for home, for family, for a coherent self and a new way of being were so great that I would put myself and anyone else at risk to get them. Though my entire life had been fashioned from overlapping stories, the wild, true thing that animated them had remained unknown to me. I was starting to feel it move under my hands, and though it terrified me, I knew that it wouldn't go away. I began to recognize that my becoming required, more than anything, being alone.

In the barn, I sat down to identify the ferns, choosing a frond and opening my guide. It was easy to tell that its leaves were pinnatifid, that its rachis was bare, but it was impossible for me to compare its sorus with the images in the book and say whether it was round or kidney-shaped, or even whether the papery indusium was attached. Looking at the plant in front of me was like encountering a different creature entirely from the one I'd been studying so diligently in the books. The sori were mounded like roe, the buttons of them irregularly shaped. It was the real thing and I was distraught, realizing that I was encountering it for the first time. There was nothing to do but keep encouraging myself to see.

After a few days, my desk was littered with a dozen dry and crumpled blades that I had not managed to name, no matter how many trips I took through my field guide. My hands felt hot as I swept them into the garbage basket near my desk. I came to Austerlitz believing that it would be simple, with all of the language I had acquired, to point to a plantlike fern and call it by its name. I felt ashamed to have thought I could simply arrive.

What is this life that I am able to skim its surface, and weave story upon story above what is real? How is it that the stories can feel so true so as to be impossible to distinguish from reality, from the feeling of the air on skin, the smell of wet earth, the emotions following in real time, one after the other? All I'd wanted was to come to know life, to come to know ferns. But the glade in my mind shattered when I encountered them as they were.

CHAPTER 25

BIG BROTHER TEXTS LITTLE SEED one afternoon while she is helping her editor get out the door. It's been three years since she's seen him. She can't remember the last time they spoke one-on-one. He landed at JFK ten minutes ago and wants to know whether he can crash with her. Little Seed stares for a moment into the editor's calendar, the familiar grid and handwriting becoming abstract for a moment, her pond struck by a stone. She had planned to go out with some college friends after work and get wasted at her regular bar, wash away the rigidness of her office life for a night. But she takes a deep breath and texts him back, yes, of course. He suggests they meet for dinner first, tells her to text him an address.

Little Seed, an adult now, wonders what it will be like. She is determined to break out of the container for this meeting, to be regarded by Big Brother as someone new. She thinks: I have spent my entire life longing for him, fantasizing about a place where we might find each other as in childhood. But she has also grown suspicious of the memories and stories given her by childhood. Perhaps she has exaggerated the sweetness of their past together; perhaps it was a story she'd relied on out of necessity, a sealed organizing bin for childhood. But now she is at the magazine. She has a new set of rules far removed from the conditions of her family home or of those with the Spider. She considers the fact that she's moved on in the world by herself, by her own choices. She knows she can be taken seriously, that she will command Big Brother's respect. She feels a flush of optimism that he is asking her for this meeting. She'll say to him, composed and generous over tangled noodles: In many ways, I was just following the example you set. At the very least, it's a chance to start new. She tells him to meet her at a soba restaurant uptown.

She finishes at the office by herself. She locks the door and tugs the handle twice. She makes sure her own desk is tidy, papers stacked, cabinets locked. She folds and refolds the cashmere throw she keeps on her chair. When she glances back at her desk, each object sits as if waiting for her return.

SHE SPOTS BIG BROTHER before he spots her, waiting in a corner booth, staring into space, smiling. He is wearing a suit she's never seen before, of textured burgundy wool, a thick tie in orange silk over a sky-blue twill dress shirt. John Donne's *Devotions* lies open in front of him, and she wonders if he's been waiting. He looks refined and handsome, with an aura of seriousness. She stands for a moment longer, lets herself admire him. She feels a little intimidated.

Little Seed, no *Medium* Seed now, inhales and crosses the shining upholstered dining room, imagining how her editor crosses the newsroom. She feels responsible for Big Brother and is happy she has worn heels. Her brain plays a reel of the scene from the outside—two siblings in beautiful clothing, certainly no confusing history between them. When she comes closer, she notices that Big Brother's suit is slightly rumpled and his hair, which he's grown to his shoulders, is gray at the temples and greasy at the ends. *Kang*, she thinks, courageously. He's grown a goatee. He meets her eyes and smiles, and she sees gray bags under his eyes.

"Hi," she says in English, trying her best to sound cheerful. She commits to English, the language of their separate worlds, hoping for a bridge.

He scrambles to his feet and wraps her in a tight hug. "Hi, Little Seed," he says back. Tears come to her eyes, hearing him address her in the diminutive. For this, she is willing to stay Little. How long has she wanted this?

"Have you been here for a long time?" she asks, gesturing at his book.

"Oh yeah, I got here in the afternoon, but they were so nice and let me stow my suitcase behind the counter," Big Brother says cheerfully. Little Seed takes in the staccato of his words, the light Chinese accent. She can't recall the last time she's spoken to him in this language and feels surprised at his foreignness. "I even took a little nap!" he says, tucking *Devotions* into a leather briefcase. Little Seed smiles too, a little bemused, thinking of Big Brother napping in a burgundy suit on the elegant leather benches, the light easing into evening. The restaurant is filled with booths of blond wood. A wooden sculpture, like the frame of a boat, hangs just above them from the ceiling so that their table feels contained and intimate. Behind Big

Brother's head is an enlarged photograph of a buckwheat field beneath blue skies.

"They say that's the actual buckwheat, in Japan, that they grow and grind up to make the soba noodles here," he says, beaming, turning around. "I'm so excited to try them."

"Me too," Little Seed says, relieved and proud to have picked a place he likes. She recalls all the clichés about what time and space can do for a relationship, senses a new ease and familiarity between them.

He asks about work, and she explains her year at the magazine. She tells him composedly that it's been an adjustment but that she's getting the hang of it. She is fully Little Seed, but in the nice way, explaining her drawings to him, feeling the warmth of his supervision. She is choosing the container this time. It feels good.

"Do you know what you want to do next?" he asks, and she feels the touch of his curiosity and she opens up about how she thought initially that she wanted to be a writer one day. But now that she's worked for a while with her editor, she's come to understand the vastness of such an operation and how it relies on so many types of people to make it run precisely. She tells him she's come to enjoy the organizational aspect of her work and thinks she's genuinely good at it. She thinks that maybe one day she'd like to pursue this, maybe even at the magazine itself.

"I'd really like to be the managing editor one day," she says, slightly terrified to articulate this wish for the first time. It's comically far off, hugely unlikely, like a kid saying she wants to be president. But she'll do anything to prolong the feeling of closeness she is in with Big Brother, desperate to expand the map of their intimacy. Big Brother is beaming, and she feels like she is dreaming, as if the shared tumult of their past has been switched off.

"That makes a lot of sense," Big Brother says, smiling. A server places bowls of noodles, tempura vegetables, and little dishes of vegetables on the table. The sesame seeds have a slight toasted sheen on their curved husks. Steam rises from clear dashi, a square of seaweed macerating in the golden broth. She looks up. Big Brother is watching her intently. She meets his gaze. "It makes a lot of sense," he continues, "because you've always been very manipulative." His eyes grow darker, his voice high and patronizing. Little Seed feels her body go cold. The server asks them if they need anything else, and she hears Big Brother's voice return to its cheerful register. They are okay, everything looks delicious.

"Okay," she says in a near whisper, suddenly returned to a familiar and terrifying landscape. He's looking at the food again, eyes wide with delight. "How is your dissertation going?" she tries tentatively. Big Brother glances up, eyes happy.

"I handed it in just before I got on the plane to JFK," he says, smiling wide, and Little Seed feels a golden interior light. She sets aside the hurt from his strange turn moments ago. She is the first to hear his good news. His trip here makes sense now. She feels a small flare of guilt that she hasn't been in touch with him along the way, sees at once the periods of uncertainty and exhaustion he must have passed through. She blames herself for not supporting him. Little Seed resigns herself to be in his story, which she understands now is about his arrival.

He leans in, across the glistening dashi, as if he is going to tell her a secret. She feels powerless in his current. She leans in too and he smiles conspiratorially.

"It's nine Chinese characters," he says.

"What do you mean, nine Chinese characters?" she asks, smiling attentively.

"My dissertation. I just turned in nine Chinese characters," he says again, now sternly, as if she is being rude or obstinate. Something ticks, clocklike, in her head.

"Well, which ones?" she says lightly. The conversation, she intuits, is now about survival. He pauses and smiles broadly.

"I can't tell you," he says, winking at her. "Only those with the highest naval clearance can read them. I classified them myself, in fact." Then he laughs. Little Seed watches joy unfold across his broad, freckled face and feels like she can't wake up. She realizes how stupid it was to think she could ever become anything but Little Seed. Who was she kidding? The lid on the container slams shut. The wooden sculpture above her head looms. The food now makes her nauseated, but she reaches for the plastic chopsticks, desperate to move the minute hand.

Big Brother pulls from his suit jacket two cheap silk sleeves, embroidered in the style of *qipaos* and ornamental pillows. He places the blue sleeve in front of her. She picks it up and removes two bamboo chopsticks, like the ones they used to use at home, when they were children.

"You should be careful of poison," he says matter-of-factly. "They're for you. Use them when you eat out." He pulls his own chopsticks from their sleeves and grins broadly as he attacks the cold dishes. She stares at the chopsticks in her hand. She suddenly feels self-conscious. What would her colleagues from the magazine think if they saw her? She imagines an assistant in the other booth, watching as she assents to her brother's world, uses these chopsticks to avoid poisoned soba.

Big Brother is eating rapidly, slurping, his face in the bowl, smiling widely between bites. Little Seed watches his fig-

ure against the field of buckwheat, in lush color, a slight blur
brushed into it by the wind.

PSYCHOTIC BREAKS PARTAKE of certain patterns. Watch
first for flat affect where it doesn't belong, an extraordinary
story relayed as distantly reported small talk, as if the person
isn't living in the words. And there is the mania, the impulsive
spending—buying a red-eye from London to New York City,
missing that flight, then immediately buying another, boarding with little more than a passport and clean socks. Delusions
of grandeur, of course, of being the smartest man at St Cath-
arine's College on historical record, of outsmarting a hapless
shrink during a psychiatric evaluation, of checking into the
emergency room at Addenbrooke's after a week of inexplicable
full-body paralysis and reemerging fully healed. Better than
healed, actually, invincible. The quiver of an oak leaf becomes
a symbol. The courteous nods and mutterings of strangers are
a call to action. There is the intense, lushly imagined paranoia
of being poisoned, followed, watched.

"I'm working for the CIA," he whispers to Little Seed as
they ride the F train back to her apartment. Fluorescence strikes
the plastic seats, blinks off the vertical grab bar. Big Brother is
standing in front of her, straddling his hard plastic suitcase, the
rich fabric of his suit crumpling over the handle of the luggage.

She follows his gaze: a dovish woman across the car absorbed in *The Invention of Nature*. It feels unfathomable that
no one in the train is party to what's happening. Little Seed
glances back at Big Brother. In February, he will turn forty.
She notices deep lines that feed the corners of his mouth, the
enlarged pores on his nose, a bead of sweat running over the

dimple of his cheek. She remembers how sweaty he used to get when he carried her on the back of his bicycle. He wipes his brow with a silk handkerchief and bends down to her.

"There's one of us here. There's one of us in Germany. And me, in England," he says. He smiles. "Do you see?" Little Seed nods vacantly. She focuses on the yellow dots of the subway map—they go dark one by one as they pass through the West Village, then SoHo, then Chinatown. He turns to her when they pass under the East River, pressing a finger to his lips.

Women shuo putonghua, he says, in Mandarin. *Let's speak in Mandarin*, a language that they have never shared. Big Brother studied it in college and Little Seed did too, partly in an attempt to emulate him. *Tamen ting by dong*, he says, gesturing around at the commuters in the car. *They can't understand.* Then he looks away, furrowing his brow, as if spotting their destination in one of the distant windows, dense and black and limitless.

Little Seed has no way of identifying Big Brother's break. All she knows is that he is presenting her with a fantasy that she cannot begin to tell him isn't true. She looks at his face, serene and knowing. Just for this train ride, just for now, it can be real. The spies, the CIA, the magic nine-character thesis, just let it be real. She sinks into his world to protect him and to protect herself. She makes herself imagine him wandering the streets of London in his suit, taking covert meetings with agents. She imagines him triumphantly turning in his thesis, nine perfect Chinese characters. She imagines a reality woven and rewoven by Big Brother's every word. For a moment, she feels something like peace.

At her apartment, she covers the living room couch with flowered sheets taken from their parents' hall closet in Tennessee. She thinks about when she will be able to call Mama, how she would even begin to explain what is happening. Big Brother drops his bag and sits on the made-up couch and says he wants to show her something. He pulls a napkin and an expensive ballpoint pen from his breast pocket, leans over her coffee table, and draws a diagram with an x-axis and a y-axis. He numbers each axis one through seven.

"This is us," he says, drawing a point where the two sevens meet on the far top-right corner of the napkin and labeling it with the Chinese character for their last name. "Seven different families in our ancestral line. Our family is in the seventh house," he says, tapping the x-axis. He gestures to the y-axis: "And seven generations of our family." Little Seed looks at him, her face growing hot. *Not like other Chinese people*, she hears Baba saying.

"Little Seed, we don't have anything to worry about," he says softly. "You don't have anything to worry about." His face lights up. "Everything is going to be fine. In fact, everything is going to be wonderful." Little Seed tries to smile back. The sureness of his calculations recalls Baba's forecasts when they were children, his certainty that they would become powerful and wealthy in specific ways. She feels the power of this fortune-telling now. She sees them both as children, denied the ability to imagine alternatives, to live outside the story. She had remained within the story because it allowed her the possibility of being loved. Whatever Big Brother had remained in it for, it had led to his ruin. Did Baba intuit that this would happen? Big Brother's reassurance, macabre as it is, seems to flood her apartment with warmth. Her chest hurts when she realizes that his wish for safety and certainty requires her to be absorbed by his delusion.

She blinks back tears and tells him they should go to bed. He smiles beatifically, and she watches him lay on top of the flowered sheet fully clothed, pulling a blanket up to his chest. "Good night, Little Seed," he says softly, watching the ceiling. "Good night, Big Brother," she replies from her bedroom. Later, sleepless, wandering into the kitchen for a glass of water, she notices that Big Brother is wide awake, staring at the ceiling, wearing an expression of utter peace.

Sleeplessness is, of course, another symptom of psychosis. Weeks later, panicked and herself unable to sleep, Little Seed makes a spreadsheet for Big Brother's symptoms. She will fill it with intricate notes about the night and day they spent together and with strange anecdotes that she collects from Big Brother's professors and his friends. She knows that she will need every detail and symptom to cut through Baba's and Mama's churning storytelling, to get Big Brother help.

The DSM-IV, WebMD, and *Psychology Today* offer hopeful, calm suggestions for diagnosing a psychotic break. They provide checklists for identifying the disappearance of a loved one, pin things to the wall with bright, certain English consonants. But they don't explain that she will feel like a sandcastle before the tide. There is the fact that as she chooses intimacy with Big Brother, she gives up a core part of her relationship with reality. And there is her desire to leave, to wish Big Brother had died outright. And reels of Mama dying in front of her again and again, Big Brother screaming at her for using his name, Baba forever slipping through her grasp, coming to her only when it suited him.

Little Seed listens to Kang's breathing that night, desperate for daylight to break. In the night, pieces of his reality wash over her: *They pay for my tailoring on Savile Row. They put me in a hospital for two weeks, and I emerged totally healed. I don't know who they are, but the money just appears. They know. They are watching.*

Little Seed imagines a team of agents in a control room under London, Big Brother's adventures, ever monitored, flickering in black and white on CCTV. His *they* frightens her more
than anything else. She, too, has begun to live within a chorus
of *they*s. *They make her feel excluded. They don't like it when she
dresses this way. They don't respect her. They need her to speak
correctly. They will finally see her if she works hard enough, if she
stays quiet, if she can be good. They know. They are watching.*
Who are they, she asks herself again and again, until her ach-
ing brain goes black.

BIG BROTHER'S DISSERTATION tells the story of Hong Xiuquan, a man of Hakkan descent, in 1850s China. Hong's mother
and father sacrifice themselves to educate him so he might pass
the imperial examination. He fails, then fails again. When he
fails a third time, he falls into a three-day delirium and hallu-
cinates a new family who lives in heaven. His new father is patient and regal and replaces his internal organs with new ones.
Hong watches as his celestial father beats Confucius to punish him for inflicting hierarchy and ritual on the Chinese people. He bestows a shining sword and shield on his new son
and, with them, the duty of ridding China of the evil that has
plagued it.

When Hong returns to Earth, he interprets his visions using
the strange pamphlets carried by Christian missionaries from
the West. He realizes he is the Christian God's second son, and
he declares himself the Celestial King. He burns the Confucian
and Buddhist texts in his home and begins to preach. His barefoot audiences grow until imperial forces take notice. They ar-
rest his followers, throw his belongings into the Yangtze River.
But the Celestial King's force only grows. He captures Nanjing,

beheading the Manchu and setting the women on fire. From atop their charred bodies, he declares the Celestial Realm of Eternal Peace.

The Celestial Realm is a utopia. No private property, no footbinding, no slavery. No opium, gambling, or prostitution. Men and women are equal and forbidden from touching one another. Within a decade, the Celestial Realm controls Southern China and the Yangtze River. Its untroubled eye turns now to Beijing and Shanghai.

But at Shanghai, Qing dynasty troops surround the forces of the Celestial Realm, defeating them, then press southward to Nanjing, Celestial Realm headquarters. That spring, on a warm and windless April morning, the Celestial King kills himself. After burying him in yellow silk near the former imperial palace, his followers do what followers do: from buildings, from doorjambs and cypress trees. With carving knives, with pitch and a borrowed flame. A month later, Qing forces close in on an eerily quiet Celestial Realm, carve up the Celestial King's body, burn it, and launch the remains from a cannon. His soul, the dissertation points out, will wander for eternity.

"GOOD MORNING, LITTLE SEED," Big Brother says, smiling sweetly. It is five, her apartment windows black and orange. He sits upright, setting their parents' folded top sheet next to him. He's dressed as he was the night before, his suit now beyond rumpled. He rests his palms on the thick wool weave of his pants and looks at her, as if waiting for direction. Little Seed is unable to believe she isn't still dreaming.

Kang, her wild-haired brother, says he wants to visit the offices of the magazine. He has a few hours to kill before he has to go. Go where? She needs to call their parents, she needs to marshal her forces, she needs an emergency exit door, but she has no idea how to begin. This version of Big Brother in the offices where she has built her new life makes her suddenly ill.

"Where are you going?" she asks, trying to change the subject. He ignores her and repeats his request. She stares back.

"What time do you go to work?" he asks her, and she feels the practicality of the question cut through the air like a bell. "I need to be there by seven," she lies, hoping the hour is too early for him to want to go. Or, if it isn't, that no one will be there when they arrive. "I have to be there before everyone else."

"Oh, nice!" he says, reaching for his wing tips. "If we leave now, we'll have time for breakfast."

TIMES SQUARE IS HUNG in a darkness and dull neon that pours down on the lone security guard sheltering at the front desk. He waves them through the turnstiles, and Big Brother lumbers through, dragging his suitcase. In the elevator, he is utterly at ease, making no effort to smooth his hair and suit. If anyone sees us, Little Seed thinks, will they know we're siblings?

They step out and Little Seed walks in front of Big Brother toward the etched glass doors, their footsteps and his suitcase wheels deafening in the empty hall. She is relieved to notice that the office is dark. She scans her badge and opens the door. Facing him again, she pretends he is a stranger and offers the pleasant, impersonal smile used for the editor's guests.

"Welcome," she hears herself say brightly. Kang brushes past her, eyes wide in the dark space. Little Seed is desperate to corral him, to tell him what he can do and cannot touch, but all she can do is chase after him, knocking lights on in his wake. He nearly runs through the magazine's mazed hallways.

He stops periodically to examine a piece of art on the wall, and Little Seed holds her breath every time, unsure of what's inside him. Will he take one off the wall, tell her matter-of-factly that it fits better in his apartment? Will he do something to hurt her?

"Where's your desk?" he asks, and she guides him through the hallways to her neatly arranged space. Her objects are waiting for her, and she feels a flush of horror—the perfectly placed stapler, the scarf folded on the back of the chair—remembering how captivated she was trying to make it perfect. She turns on her desk lap and sits down in her desk chair, as if it were any other day.

"Okay, so, this is work!" Little Seed says, waving her hands frantically over the papers on her desks, miming work, hoping it will signal he has to go. But she knows she's unconvincing in that empty, half-lit cavern. Big Brother tilts his suitcase to the floor and unzips its hard case. He props the lid open against her cubicle wall and retrieves from yet another silk pouch a gleaming digital camera.

"For Mama and Baba," he says, holding the camera, mask-like, against his face. Move to the left, his free hand says. She feels a dull ache in her eyes as the flash goes off.

When the world comes back into focus, Kang is rummaging again through his suitcase. He digs out a cylinder in gift paper. "This is for you," he says. "It's a Christmas gift." It's a pencil holder made of luminous red-orange wood. The grain shimmers in the light; a vein of chestnut meanders around its waist. Little Seed turns it over in her hands, watching the colors shift in the lamplight.

"It's from China," Big Brother says. "I bought it when I was doing research there for my dissertation. I thought you might want one for your first adult job." Little Seed thanks him and in the same moment is overtaken by anger and shame directed, somehow, at the pencil holder. She is ashamed of it, the innocent pencil holder, staring back at her: I didn't make him this way. You think I asked to be chopped down? Little Seed looks up. The sun has broken free of Brooklyn. Kang is striding toward Editors' Row.

"That's where the editors sit," she says a bit wildly, pink sunlight streaming through the windows of the editors' offices. "Well, then, I definitely want to see that," he calls out to her. She panics, wondering if a lone editor is somehow here. She checks that the door to her editor's office is locked, tugging once, and runs after him.

Anxiety about being seen here, of disturbing the air, floods her when she enters Editors' Row. But this is replaced by dread: Big Brother is nowhere to be found. She walks faster, stopping and peering into each of the editors' offices, realizing as she does that she has always been so nervous of them that she's barely noticed the trinkets on their desks, the photos on their walls. Now she notices families posing in front lawns, children's untidy handwriting, postcards from Belize, life-dust. How tender it all feels: she is angry. How distant the editors and the assistants have made themselves from her—she knows she will feel their detachment again when the office is repopulated. But for now, she understands that there is no real difference between her and an editor. Why had she believed that anyone was more sophisticated, smarter, more knowing, *better*? And here is Kang, sitting in the office of the senior editor who has always intimidated her the most. He hasn't learned her name, even after a year of interactions. She stops at the threshold of the sliding door that Big Brother has thrown open.

She watches, frozen, as he pulls books off the shelves and flips through them, humming as he does, making little delighted noises here and there. He reshuffles the books, checks the integrity of the desk, spins a paperweight in his hand, leafing through a stack of papers neatly collected in a pile. It is a manuscript for a story that hasn't yet been published, and Little Seed feels her trepidation dissolve into longing. How easily he picks those pages up, as if they belong to him. His head is inclined, upper lip slightly moist, eyes clear and piercing, and she knows she is witnessing a kind of freedom she doesn't yet understand. Her neck grows hot, and her ears wait for the sound of footsteps.

And so what? she thinks to herself. Should she back down, shrink before a mighty editor? Why? These editors, the assistants, this magazine, they have created a ridiculous world with its semivisible shifting barriers. Thirty minutes after dawn and eight minutes before her editor arrives, Big Brother packs up his suitcase and begins dragging it toward the elevator.

CHAPTER 26 \\\\ *Onoclea sensibilis*

I GAVE UP ON the *Peterson* guide. I had failed and felt embarrassed about how little I actually knew. Fronds of wasted paper filed in my trash can. I thought about the fern society and wondered if I should have given up on it so early because of my discomfort—if I'd stuck it out, maybe I wouldn't be at such a loss now.

But then again, the feeling of grappling for guidance from someone else, of looking for the right way to be . . . what had it ever gotten me? A family that manipulated my sense of safety in order to ease their own pain? A boyfriend who required me to drink tea from a sock and thought walnuts were poison? Worse, I was starting to see how my fixation with a correct story had led me to hurt others, how my insistence on being led along by the right person turned the world and the people around me into objectives.

Much later, I would come to see that there's no such thing as a correct interpretation of a fern; every guide is an imprecise expression of a single perspective, a private language between a person and a plant. You can't slip into a field guide without first understanding your own private language with ferns. Using a field guide requires translation—what's a cup-shaped indusium to me might be a cuff link to another eye. But I didn't have a freestanding relationship to the world yet; I didn't even have a self, really, or at least not one that I could find. But relationships, like rivers, just keep moving, inexorably and at their own pace. I felt ruined and out of control in the forests around Austerlitz. But without knowing it, I was learning how to see the ferns and, by extension, myself.

When the sun began to honey in the late afternoon, I would leave the barn and return to the woods. I'd start by crossing the yellowing field of hay surrounding the barn. I'd cross to the gravel road flanked by a fern I suspected was *Onoclea sensibilis*, the sensitive fern. It was the only fern I had reliably identified. It just looked so much like its picture. The sensitive fern has blue-green fronds and resembles a child's painting of a fern. When held up to the light, its veins make a delicate mosaic.

Later, I would learn that *Onoclea* is native to both the Eastern Seaboard of the United States as well as the northeastern coast of China, an artifact of the early Tertiary, when land bridges between the continents allowed species to migrate. (Another relic of the circumboreal forest: redwoods are native to Coastal California and Hubei, China.) It made me sentimental to think of this fern in two parts of the world. I kept its dou-

bled range like a secret, untouched by story, going down the
road in the growing blue dusk.

ON THE EDGE OF THE WOODS fell a thick grove of ferns, in
seafoam green, the branching of their tips so intricate that they
draped silkily across one another. A down of silver hairs grew
from each leaf, and each blade stood upright like a fan wedged
into the earth. There were hundreds growing in that clearing,
rippling in the autumn wind. I crossed the meadow, hands
among their sericin tips, and was overcome with the odor of
sun-warmed earth. I thought of long days in the woods of Tennessee, of green shoots in the black topsoil of my mother's
garden.

I held a blade to my nose as I crossed the field back to the
barn. A perfume of pure green—the hairy crispness of tomato
plants, a high canopy in light. The yard on hands and knees,
the bright thrill of dirt-red beetles, the terror of the hourglass
on the belly of a black spider in her web, white-and-yellow
honeysuckle dressing a dirt path, craggy opalescent pieces of
quartz lodged in the earth's red clay, run under an outdoor tap
to see the facets sparkle in the light, the fireflies' pulse against
the orange nylon of a tent wall, my brother helping me up a
rocky incline, both of us in search of a waterfall, his palms
waiting beneath me.

CHAPTER 27 \\\\

BIG BROTHER HAS TO GO, has to check on the other agents employed by the CIA, whispers their initials to Little Seed as he holds the elevator doors. He promises to see her at Christmas. She wishes at once she could ask him to stay. The elevator descends, and she runs back to her desk and calls Mama. Explaining Kang's delusions in her unsophisticated Shanghainese is like painting with her pinkies.

I just saw Big Brother, and he has a problem, she says on the phone. *He said that he did things that I know he didn't. He left, and I don't know where he's going. I am very afraid.*

Mama sounds concerned, but she admonishes Little Seed for being sensitive. She says that Big Brother is probably just very stressed and tired. Mama says she knows in the future to keep Big Brother and Little Seed apart if it creates such a problem. Little Seed suppresses the humiliation of being misunderstood and tries again. She tells Mama that Big Brother is acting strangely, and it isn't a question of her perception. Mama should be as frightened as she is. Mama's voice becomes hushed, and she says she will speak to Baba about it. Little Seed tells her she is going to call Cambridge to ask what Big Brother's adviser knows, whether others have noticed he is a CIA agent.

Later that afternoon, Baba sends Little Seed an email in English. Little Seed feels immediately on guard, knowing he's written it in this language so that he can be sure she will understand. He instructs her to be careful and not accuse the professor of anything, not to reveal that there may be something wrong with Big Brother. The professor is of a high class position, he says, and she wouldn't necessarily know how to talk to him. He tells her she should approach the situation as if she were a concerned little girl asking after her brother.

Reading this, Little Seed gives up, in a flash of all-consuming rage, the story she has been telling herself her entire life. The magazine doesn't matter, her native proficiency in English doesn't matter. So long as she is complicit in the telling of Baba's story, she will always be here, in this cavernous, light-filled office, her father reminding her in broken English to remember her place, to ingratiate herself at all costs.

All she sees now is Big Brother broken before her. The desire to be respected, to belong, to be safe has required so many transactions of each of them that there is nothing left. Baba's story, Mama's story, the story she believed about herself feels increasingly remote, a landmass at a distant horizon, a book other people read. But I'm not only this book or these pages. This is my life, and I can't leave it. And I'm fucking sick of living twice. I want to be here without casting twenty years into the past every time I feel danger. I'm sick of placating narcissists who remind me of my dad. I'm sick of protecting people like my mom who expect me to put their hurt and their fear before my own pain. I'm sick of longing for the protection of people like my brother who are too unwell to care for anything. And most of all, I'm sick of how much I still love them, can't help but love them. Putting loving them before living.

And I'm sick of my desperation to fit all of these emotions into a readable narrative so someone will understand me and make the space between us safe. I've spent my entire life translating myself into a language the outside world speaks, to prove that I'm here in sentences and paragraphs and words, obsessed with telling, worried that no one will relate unless I lure them through the story so they can hurt how I hurt, so they can remember for the rest of their lives some small detail—an engagement ring, a pair of chopsticks, the pinnule of a fern. Who the fuck is this for, anyway? Is it also humiliating for you to try to be alive?

CHAPTER 28 \\\\ The Dying Fern

AFTER MY BROTHER LEFT, I was alone in my apartment with a fern that was dying before I knew what it was. At the time, all I knew about ferns was that they like humidity and light, and my little studio was dry and dingy. I took to changing its placement around the room from week to week, trying to catch the sun. I set its pot on a plate of water and river rocks and misted its delicate fronds twice a day. Though new tendrils came up all the time, it wasn't long before the fronds browned at the ends and dried to paper.

I had bought the plant unlabeled. I liked its strangeness. Its shape dispersed in long hanging lines, patches of kelly green, not unlike parsley or cilantro. Each stem resolved into a hand of five leaves, their edges saw-toothed. Sometimes, the center leaf would erupt at its tip into a crown of smaller irregular leaves, as if it were attempting, midgrowth, to try something else.

Only later, as it neared death, I began to wonder what it was. I never found out—I thought it might have been a moonlight fern, *Pteris cretica*, named for a band of silver that runs down the pinnae of mature leaves, but my fern didn't have this. I became absorbed by the knowledge that ferns are a different type of organism from seed plants.

I knew there was something incorrect about the way I thought about plants. I thought I might be able to save my fern if I could find and correct this. I devoured books on the biology, cultural history, and classification of ferns. I collected field guides, drilling myself on the shapes of pinnules, sori, rhizomes.

Ferns don't die all at once. Their fronds reach inward, papering from tip to root. I kept the mystery plant in its pot, watching it shrivel and fold away. A fern in reverse. The end arrives in its many moments, the curling of every leaf into itself until it is a dark wisp, until it's anything at all: a stick of incense, a crease in the binding of a book, a shadow.

I SAW MY BROTHER'S GHOST in Times Square. He was in a coffee shop, hanging on to the metal handle of the front door, screaming at people, haranguing. He wore baggy green cargo pants and an oversized blue T-shirt. His hair was long and dull. My body recognized his temples, the broad cheekbones of his face, the bulging eyes, and I was crying as I ran toward him, wondering how I would get him into a taxi, wondering how I would carry him home. How had he gotten up here?

I was thinking in Shanghainese and I heard my voice soften and pitch high. *Big Brother, Big Brother, Big Brother*, I begged in our shared dialect. Imagining him looking at me, imagining him calling me. But he didn't hear me. I wandered close enough to see the sweat running down his cheek, I was still begging for him to hear me, to hear the words coming out of his mouth. I reached my hands out for his arm, ready to tug on it like I had when I was small, knowing he had me. He turned and stared at me from inside another man's face, another man's body. The man paused his ranting and studied me, genuinely curious, outdone. I apologized in English and fled, wiping my cheeks with my palms.

By then, Kang was home with my parents, recovering. Time was again lost between us, but Mom told me he spent every day sleeping in a dark room. I expected heartbreaking news all the time—an assault charge, a violent thing with the police, a borrowed handgun, doorjambs and cypress trees. So I tried to stop thinking about Kang and then about my family at all. And I went back to drinking, more seriously now, every evening.

One day, Mom called to tell me that my brother had bought a fish. His bathtub was now an aquarium, filled with plastic plants and flowers. He had done his research and bought the right kind of filter. She said the fish was beautiful, vivid red, and that it responded to my brother's voice. She took care of it when he left the house for a few days, and when it heard her voice, it would swim out from under its plastic leaf, knowing it would be fed. In the moments before it emerged, she feared it wouldn't.

THE MYSTERY FERN DIED and my brother remained unwell. I came to see my life as a series of failures. I had spent all of it devoted to the insecurities and desires of others, which was of course a particularly terrible way of devoting my life to my own insecurities and desires. I couldn't seem to stop. I kept re-arranging whatever was in front of me into a wall between myself and the world ahead. I think I didn't see myself as real, as something to be held or challenged or loved.

I left the magazine, I left the old stories, carried the dead fern out the front door.

IV. GHOST STORY

tree fern

A CIRCADIAN MEMORY OF Punta Cometa each morning before sunrise, the narrow sandy path winding through a thicket of desert trees. Lizards dart underfoot; birds ping around, check on each branch. Where the trees fall away, the path disappears over a cliff. The sky and sea appear. I shuttle carefully down the dusty drop and across a land bridge to a heap of sun-bleached limestone against the aquamarine sea. The limestone plateau is carpeted by a green down of desert plants and grasses. The steep sides, plunging into the ocean, are striated by glittering pink, gold, and ocher bands. Fishermen perch in outcrops, casting and reeling. Sometimes there is a catch. After the sun rises, they pick their way back across the stone faces, cooler in one hand, bucket in the other.

The path winds its way haphazardly around the mountain.

As I ascend, the limestone becomes lush with spiked vines, short palms, and tall grasses—Mexican analogies to the red clover, thistle, and wild carrot of my childhood. I am looking for ferns but never find any—not on the coast, not in the dry season. Instead, I find soft pink foxtails and stars of white flowers in moss, a small succulent vine that trails above me against the warm white stone. As I circle higher and higher, the ocean unrolls before me. Below, beaches surround Punta Cometa, some dotted with umbrellas and plastic chairs, some deserted and rocky, black seaweed billowing under the surf.

The side where the peninsula dissolves into the ocean is a steep drop. Looking over the edge makes my stomach light. The water down there, a shallow and sun-shot teal, shatters and heals over the rocks. At high tide, the waves mount and their blue deepens. Some pool into the shoals like cooling fog; others explode against the rocks, their spray carried by the wind to my arms and face.

When the tide is low, a huge bowl emerges from the limestone. A whale calf could curl up inside it. Water enters it continuously, slapping the sides of the basin, making eddies in black, indigo, and aquamarine. The whirlpool is alluring, set like a big magnet against the mountain. Once, I shuffled down the cliff like a crab until I reached the worn stone floor, soaked black from salt water. I balanced myself on the edge, watching the water settle until the foam subsided and the water clarified. Before long, another wave surged in, and I screamed and laughed, completely drenched. There is mystery and danger in the unseen undertow, the churning. From high above, I think: I am that whirlpool. Here is where I am embodied. There is the inevitability, the machination, the pull.

At the very end of the path, you can't see the whirlpool. The blue of the ocean and of the sky dissolve into each other.

Near the edge, there is a stone shaped like a saddle. I straddle it, placing my hands on the hot rock, watching the neon-red disk of the sun crest the horizon. I watch it fade to white as it ascends, turning the sky cerulean, lavender, baby blue. I fill with salt air and become empty. Time is plain and obvious here. The quality of sunlight shifts every moment, the sky expands and changes textures.

I was there to grieve. But I didn't know exactly why or how. I told myself I was mourning my brother, but that couldn't be correct. He was still here in the world, still in my parent's home, lying in a darkened room. What I was actually doing was looking at the Pacific Ocean and noticing the sun striking some otherwise invisible thing in the distance—a raft, a piece of debris, a sounding whale. I could make out only the way it would tug at the surface of the sea, the water boiling at the point of contact, then healing at once, just the same as everything else, back to horizon, to the surface, to the whole.

I HAD BOUGHT A ONE-WAY TICKET to the coast of Oaxaca, a state in southern Mexico, because I knew it was famous for its density of ferns. My plan was to hang out for a while on the coast in a town called Mazunte, reading and swimming in the ocean. When I was ready, I would go and search for ferns.

I stayed in a clutch of nine cement bungalows, white boxes perched on a ridge of rain forest over a beach where leatherback turtles laid their eggs. To the west of the beach was Punta Ventanilla, a rock formation comprising a square opening of sky. The thunder of the waves drifted up the ridge into my bungalow. Now and again, I smelled salt.

My space was simple—a large room enclosed by three perforated brick walls on a thick concrete slab. The south face of the room was open to the jungle. Louvered wood doors could be slid into place in the event of storms or mosquitoes. Otherwise, it was a wall of sky over the shifting shadows of tree branches, cacti, and the boulders that littered the jungle floor. There was an open-air shower and a sink in one corner and a poster bed in the center of the room swathed in mosquito gauze.

I passed the sweltering afternoons in my bungalow reading books on ferns and journaling on a small daybed, noting things I wanted to remember: the Victorian fern craze, the strangeness of fern reproduction. Spore to haploid gametophyte, gametophyte to diploid sporophyte. I'd take cold showers every few hours and tie my hair back with a faded red bandana.

I felt moved, too, to recall my childhood, to record as much as I could remember about my family and my brother. It felt urgent to remember everything I had tried until then to forget. As I wrote, I saw how resentful I was toward my brother for his lack of attention, the way he hadn't fulfilled my expectations of what I thought an older brother should be. I saw how angry I had become when he wouldn't protect me, when he refused to keep me safe or make me feel special. And I saw how cruel it was to call these expectations love. I'd made up a story that made my brother responsible for the person I wanted to be. This, among other things, relieved me of the terrifying responsibility of making my own decisions about life.

I had known love as a list of requirements—to be subservient to my parents and my brother, to stop feeling pain, to grow my hair long and be pretty, to wear beautiful shoes, to stop eating, to drink tea from a sock, to come to work early, to speak excellent English. Love was something lent to you by others when you gave them what they wanted.

I sat in the three-sided room in the jungle and tried to write a new story about love and about my brother, one about care rather than security or expectation. To do so, I had to write out the false stories, and in so doing render them brittle as a dying fern. And as they dissolved in front of me, one after another, I wept like a child, feeling my sense of reality move in the jungle around me. I knew that abandoning my childhood notions about my brother meant a different brother on the other side.

I thought so much about love in those days. I found myself crying unpredictably, sobbing ugly and openmouthed as I hiked Punta Cometa in the mornings or pulling my bandana over my face in town in the afternoon looking for mangoes.

I became more and more comforted by ferns. Did you know that the sperm of ferns is corkscrew-shaped? Or that one water-dwelling genus, *Azolla*, has been used for centuries to fix nitrogen in rice paddies? Green fronds in the flooded fields. They had anchored me to the world, to Oaxaca, to this grief.

ENGLISH AND CHINESE WERE PRECIOUS on the coast. When I found either—in a shop, in a bar, on an early morning boat ride—I'd make a picnic of it. But after a few weeks, I began to prefer Spanish because I spoke almost none of it. I could see everyone around me bare of what they said or meant to say. I would draw nearer to the eyes, the lines in a face, the little gestures of a body.

At the same time, I felt a deep solitude, the unknown days before me like a crevasse. Every few days, I would indulge in despair: Would I still have a life when I returned? What had I done? My emotional landscape remained riddled with craters and shell holes, and I couldn't predict when I would fall into one and find myself in darkness. Each time I vanished into myself and returned, I found the earth and sea of Mazunte waiting beneath me, palms up. It didn't matter if I spent most of the week crying. There was, above, the astonishing sunset throwing a dense orange light over Mazunte and me.

Each night, I lay on the cooling concrete ledge and looked up at the stars, recollecting the emotions of the day. The lush violet glitter of the Milky Way. Frog song and the distant sea.

I'M PRETTY SURE THAT Adriana noticed me because I was starving and desperate for company most mornings after my hike from Punta Cometa. She managed the *posada* and prepared breakfast in the late mornings. I would always arrive before the others, early enough to drink three mugs of the weak Oaxacan coffee Adriana boiled in a tin. By then, the open-air kitchen was crackling with hot oil and thick with the steam of boiling salsa, onion skin and tomato tops littering the counter. At first, she'd shoo me away to the long table outside the kitchen that overlooked the faraway sea. But eventually, she let me perch on a counter with a book while she cooked. She wore bright colors and chunky jewelry, her large almond eyes in lines of expert kohl, no matter how sweltering it was.

Most mornings, we listened to the radio. She'd translate our astrological forecasts into English—romantic love was never in the stars for me that summer. Adri flipped her long black hair to punctuate a point and sighed in exasperation about the heat, about how slow construction had been on the pool, about Mateo, her invincible son, losing his *chanclas* for the third time that summer. She said she was studying for the law school entrance exam and wanted to open a café serving authentic Oaxacan moles in the city and design her own posada here on the coast.

We'd linger over lavish breakfasts with Mateo, Negra the

dog, and whichever guests passed through that day. Fried tortillas folded into golden ears and submerged in red salsa or refried beans against lacy-edged fried eggs, salted steaks, and paper-thin tortillas, hand pressed and toasted by the abuelas in town. Stews of tomatillo, zucchini, and fresh white cheese, *chuletas* caramelized at their edges and topped with fresh tomatoes, onions, and chiles. A salsa laced with chile oil so hot I had to excuse myself from the table. And always pitchers of icy agua fresca made with pineapple or mangos or limes with fresh mint.

Eventually, I started talking to Adri about the ferns. I told her that's why I'd come, that I wanted to learn about them. I knew they were in Oaxaca, but I wasn't sure where to go or how to go about it since I didn't have any Spanish and didn't know anyone. Maybe it was enough to just stay on the coast and rest. I pulled up a picture of a sensitive fern on my phone to show her what I meant. "*Helecho*," she whispered, squinting and pulling the screen apart with her fingers.

"Oh, they aren't here, not now," she said, putting my phone down and raising her coffee cup to her face, thinking. "In August or September, it's all green, everything." I imagined the heart-shaped leaves of a philodendron vine descending from the palapa, lush monstera and cereus creeping under the table with their enormous white flowers. "You'd love it. But now"—she waved her hand toward the brittle, anemic bushes along the dirt path—"nothing." My heart sank a bit, but I'd already suspected that I wouldn't see any ferns here on the coast. It was all sand and salt.

"But actually, Wei," she continued, turning to me, "if you are still here in May, there's a *feria* in Oaxaca City. Maybe you can go." I asked her what she meant. "It's like a fair . . . for plants." She puckered her lips and squinted, homing in on some faraway idea, then loosed a stream of words and gestures, all Spanish. I let it wash over me, and she returned to English. "It's like Jurassic Park, you know? Like something from a long time ago. But there will be many of your helechos there."

Maybe it was a street fair, I thought. Hot dogs and corn. Or a conference. A fluorescent warehouse, fabric booths, Boston ferns and pothos. Neither option sounded particularly appealing. "Whatever!" Adri broke in, as if by way of explanation. "You'll love it. I'll find you Fernando's information and you can write to him and you can go." I said okay and helped her clear the dishes.

CHAPTER 30 \\\\

ONE MORNING, A TATTOOED WELDER from Vancouver with a platinum buzz cut sat down to breakfast. He wore tiny oval sunglasses tinted yellow and an unbuttoned silk shirt. He was good-looking and spoke in sweeping generalizations, sounding a bit revelatory even when he was not. But he was sweet, and I felt myself soften toward him. The welder was, like me, in Mazunte for an unspecified amount of time and for reasons he mostly avoided. He had a girlfriend and a Harley in Vancouver. Most of the people I met on the coast were roughly as lonely as I was. Later that morning, we walked to the local language school, got rejected, and wandered into town. We landed at a surf shack, drinking kombucha and watching the waves.

A white woman with an enormous mane of curly black hair and flowing silk pants landed at our table and, without pre-

amble, diagnosed my Ayurvedic disposition. I was clearly of
vata build—anxious, restless, and talkative. That hurt my feelings a little until she made intense eye contact with the welder
and told him throatily that he, like her, had a *pata* disposition:
burning with fire, passion, and virility. The welder smiled
sheepishly, and I let my attention wander, observing the street
grow busier as the shadows shortened.

Like a lot of villages along the coast of Oaxaca, Mazunte
was a hippie town, influenced by cycles of white expats and
backpackers who came for the beaches and occasionally stayed.
Puerto Escondido hosted famous surfing competitions at Zica-
tela Beach. Zipolite was Mexico's only legal nude beach, established by European hippies in the 1970s. White people in sa-
ris and dreadlocks, chakras and yoga retreats, hemp, roving
bands of freegans. But the coast was rich with mestizo and indigenous cultures, too. From where I was sitting, I could see
a side street lined by comals smoking with handmade gordi-
tas stuffed with beans or chicharrones. There were brightly
painted tiendas selling fresh fruit, meat hanging from glassless
windows. Women hawked *guisados* redolent in plastic bowls,
and children in traditional embroidered shirts teased packs of
street dogs whose ribs stood out under their fur.

Historically, Mazunte was made famous by the meat and
eggs of turtles. Twentieth-century hunters and traders were
drawn by the diversity of species that came to the beaches to
breed. A slaughterhouse was established in town to process turtle meat. But regulations were eventually passed to protect the
turtles, who were then on the edge of extinction. The town has
since been rehabilitated and turned into a place for ecotourism.
On Avenida Principal there now stands a museum dedicated to
turtles. But I'd still catch whispers of limones blancos, turtle
eggs traded illegally and eaten raw with lime and salt.

I waved at Francisco, the coconut-flecked flan seller. He walked down the streets every afternoon selling perfect coconut flan out of a metal bucket. He would chatter at me in Spanish while I ate, venting his Hawaiian shirt with a free hand, taking my empty can. Today, he sat down and added his Spanish to the ongoing Ayurvedic summit. Even though I couldn't understand anything, I felt a sudden and invincible feeling of togetherness.

In the sun-fired street, I heard a familiar voice calling to us and saw Adriana sipping from a can of Tecate on the porch of a cheerfully colored bar nearby. She waved us over. I stuck my tongue out at Mateo, and the welder took a seat next to her. Adri urged me to sit and have a drink, and though a part of me resisted, stubborn about my reading and writing, I realized that I wanted to let these people creep into my life.

Adri told us that her friends, a couple from Monterrey, had just opened the bar. It was, with great pride, the only establishment in Mazunte that served *alitas*, wings, though they'd already sold out of their entire stock and had asked Adri if she might pick up a few frozen bags the next time she was in Pochutla. As the afternoon cooled into evening, the couple from Monterrey, Roberto and Rosa, joined us bearing mezcal. They were young, gregarious punks in piercings and black tees, shuttling back and forth from our table to the business of running a bar. During a lull, Roberto, who spoke English, showed me around the still-bare space—the tiny kitchen, the newly installed swings overlooking the street on the deck, and the tent on the roof where he and Rosa slept each night.

Downstairs, the welder was at the counter, chatting with Rosa about her tattoos, so I was alone with Adriana as the night fell and the floodlights outside the bar blinked on. We were drunk. She put on my ponderous New York architect

glasses, laughing at their false seriousness. How sophisticated
I'd thought the thick black frames made me look when I picked
them out while I was at the magazine; how incongruous they
now seemed with my disintegrating cutoffs and sports bra. She
returned them to me gingerly and, casting a sideways glance at
the welder, whispered, "Wei, I *like* him."

"Really?"

"Yes," she said. She leaned back and folded her arms: "I *really* like him." She told me that they had met at a bar the night
before and had flirted and danced until very late. She'd per-
suaded him to move into our posada. "He says he has a girlfriend," she said. After a beat of silence, she gave me a conspiratorial look and threw her head back, laughing. I glanced
up in time to see the welder making his way back to us. Adri
smoothed her hair and changed the conversation to helechos,
possibly for my benefit.

Near the end of the night, Adriana withdrew a wrinkled receipt out of her wallet and copied an email from her phone onto
the back of it. "Here, Fernando. Write to him. I think it costs a
thousand pesos or something. He will tell you." I thanked her
and tucked the receipt (for chanclas) into my pocket. When I
looked up, Adri and the welder were locked in intimate conversation, giggling. I took the cue and mounted the quiet dark
trail back to the posada. Overhead, the moon was bright and
blurry.

A GRAY-AND-BROWN PUPPY, barely the size of my open
hand, came to breakfast the next morning, rolling around on
the concrete of the breakfast palapa, squeaking. He was wearing a tiny yellow-and-blue soccer jersey and was so small that
I was almost afraid to touch him. Adriana and the welder were

bleary-eyed and maybe still a little drunk and explained to me that they'd found the puppy at a party they'd gone to after I'd left the bar. They told me they had named him Seven, an inside joke they were too embarrassed to explain.

"Did you email Fernando yet?" Adri asked me, suddenly alert. Of course I hadn't. "Wei," she whined, drawing out my name into three notes. "This afternoon, we're going to the secret beach," she said, picking Seven up, puckering her lips in his face. "Write to Fernando after breakfast, and then come back and we go." I was part of her *we*, I noticed.

I flew back to my room and surveyed my laptop, books, journals, remembering the narrative with which I'd arrived in Mazune, of quietude and grief. Just a few days ago I had been lost in that story, spiraling in my loneliness. I surveyed the daybed, the little writing desk, the great open window of sky and felt grateful to know they would be there when I returned. And yet, a pang of sadness, a nervousness that my world was expanding before I was ready.

I changed and ran to the little internet café off Avenida Principal, where I hacked together a note in Spanish to Fernando. I picked up a bottle of water and hurried back to the posada, where I joined Adriana, the welder, the couple from Monterrey, and Francisco, the flan seller, in a hulking, half-destroyed green truck, half salt by weight.

I sat in the middle of the back seat of the truck between Adriana and Rosa, present and calm and without much to say. The car was a cacophony of Spanish, English, and the welder's Albertan French. We raided a supermarket for chuletas, onions, peppers, potato chips, and beer. We devoured carnitas at an open-air tent where the air shimmered above vats of pig parts drowned in golden oil. Francisco, bits of sugar in his hair, teased me wherever we went, chattering at me in Spanish and making wild hand gestures. Adri finally said what was obvious: "Wei, I think he *likes* you."

We joined the Mexican freeway, wind and radio filling the cab. The welder drove and Francisco directed him, finger against the windshield at every turn. The roads shrank and roughened; the jungle grew thicker and wilder around us. Rocks began to lurch and slide under our tires. Just as I had begun to worry that we'd get a flat or break an axle, Francisco held up his hand and the welder let off the gas. We rolled to a stop, surrounded by rock and ravine and jungle, but I smelled salt. Everyone clambered out and began ransacking the truck.

Francisco led us down through the jungle and onto a steep rocky path, our flip-flops more inadequate by the moment. Picking our way down, we arrived at a clearing of sky, and then, after a steep drop, a small white sand beach, just big enough for the six of us, in a horseshoe cove shaded by the cliff we'd just scrambled down. "Playa del Muerto," the welder told me, in a mysterious tone, though the only thing deadly about it appeared to be the entry. We dropped our robust rough coolers and towels in the sand, and Francisco made us follow him through the shallows of the shore and into a cluster of boulders. We sidled over natural riprap and climbed a ledge where we could see into the cove's clear water from above. Shoals of yellow and blue fish flickered in the current. Francisco called to us from the other side of the ledge, pointing out a hole in the stone whose edges had been worn smooth by pounding waves. Sticking my head in, I could hear the ocean rushing in down below and, in the air around my head, a steady low note, as if whistled very far off and right in my ear.

I looked up, delighted. Francisco was nodding at me. "Ahhh," he said, nodding his head, his eyes romantic. "*La canción del mar.*" He put his hand over his heart and looked at me. "*Esto es para ti,"* he said. I froze, unsure of how to respond. *"Para ti,"* he insisted, pointing at me and eyes earnest. I laughed, told him *"No entiendo,"* and scurried back to the shore, where the couple from Monterrey was putting on snorkels and flippers. I spent the rest of the afternoon bubbling around the cove, chasing neon fish and silver barracuda, sharing a joint on the beach, and passing around bags of chile-and-lime potato chips. Roberto invented a game in which he would pause the conversation and ask me what I thought they were speaking about in Spanish. Whatever I said would make the group roar, everyone toasting my can of Modelo and patting me on the arm.

When the sun was setting, I swam out to a large rock and hoisted myself onto it, dipping my feet into the water and observing pale angelfish circle around, nipping at the seaweed threads that grew from the submerged stone. I breathed in the salt air, the warm sting of aftersun on my skin, and thought about how I had come into a little community.

My thoughts wandered to my brother. I remembered again how I used to think of him as a guide into the world. What would he think of me now, allowing myself to be captured by this ocean, this place, these people? The colors of the horizon softened as I reflected on all the stories I had written about my brother. I understood that the man I had made my brother into—the adventurous one, the one animated by self-possession, with the bravery to leave—was someone I'd invented in order to dream of another kind of life. This life was not my brother's to give me, to lead me into.

I looked out on the water, at the limitless point in the distance that I knew encompassed this moment and the rest of the world, the stars and Milky Way invisible overhead, and felt a brief sorrow for the texture of the world, for the beauty and complexity and feeling I had missed because I had been waiting for someone—my brother, my family, my friends, a romantic partner, a job—to allow me it. The clouds turned purple-pink over the setting sun, and I watched these colors ripple on the water. The sky disappeared into the ocean, and I found the faint line of the emerging moon. A breeze raised goose bumps on my arm.

At the beach, the others had built a bonfire. We roasted chuletas and peppers on sticks and ate them in fire-softened tortillas. The truck got stuck in the rocks on our way back; Roberto and the welder spent an hour working to push it back onto the road. I needed to pee so badly I almost started crying. Fortunately, on the way home, a bar emerged from the darkness, and we stopped.

Over Tecate, I asked Adriana to translate to Francisco that I wasn't romantically interested in him. He clutched his head in his hands and mock wailed, *"Bienvenidos a la* Friendzone!" then shook my hand like I'd been a worthy opponent. I nodded off in the back seat the rest of the ride while the welder drove and the Mexicans scream-sang torch songs with the radio. I melted into Adri's shoulder as the car beams roved over the steep ascent back to our posada and clambered heavily into bed, warm and drunk and salt-stung, looking once at the flickering night sky before a deep and dreamless sleep.

A FEW DAYS LATER, I reported to a saltwater pool by the beach in town. I was there for a session of aguahara, a kind of water therapy that the welder had recommended to me, a little teary-eyed over his eggs. He said it was meditative and comforting, possibly even a little psychedelic.

Here's the thing about Mazunte: you arrive thinking you're here for *authentic* Mexican culture, not the hippie gringo backpacker shit with its obsidian yoni eggs. The fruitarians are an eyesore, and you don't like the taste of kombucha. You *hate* macramé.

You underestimate the culture. It is grinding and ubiquitous and invincible in its grinning insistence. Something about the surf and the sun, your emotional thinness . . . you're outnumbered. Before long, you're locked into conversation with a stranger on the street about the enneagram and the Major Arcana. And you're, in my case, holding the hand of a tall white woman with mermaid hair by the saltwater pool so you can connect before you do water therapy.

"What's your name?" she asked me from one kind foot above. Her hands and her big brown eyes were soft. The waves crashed in the distance.

"I'm Wei," I said.

"That name has special significance for you, doesn't it?" she asked. The gall. Whose name doesn't have special significance *for them*? It's like telling someone that their childhood involved growth. Here we are: a woo-woo white lady holding the hand of an Asian girl and telling her that her Chinese name holds a "special meaning." There was still time for us to do the *Flower Drum Song*. Was I going to have to reassure her that, actually, a lot of white women age well too? Does this bitch want her own chapter? I'll fucking do it!

But in fact I felt safe. The feeling of her hand holding mine was nice. And, credit to cold readers everywhere, she was right about my name. I broke down and began to cry redundantly into the saltwater pool. I told her everything. That she was right and my name was very special. That I had chosen it for myself, that it had been my brother's, who now went by Kang, yes, like *King Kong*. That I felt I had lost him, and in losing him, I had lost myself.

When I was done speaking, she took my hand and led me into the deep end of the pool. I closed my eyes, and she gathered me in her arms, my body floating in the water, and spun me slowly in a circle. The sun played over my eyelids, amber stars and red pulses. She asked if I was ready, and when I squeezed her hand, she floated me out by the legs, holding my feet tightly. Then she unfurled my body gently until I was stem straight. She dragged me in a circle, in an undulating wave. I caught my breath each time my face surfaced. I was weightless, emptied. I cried the entire time, throat burning, tears mingling with the other salt water.

I think letting go must be an unconscious act, like formation, a process one isn't able to observe, really. I had wanted so badly to see the grief pour out of me, to count and weigh it on the way out. But what I felt was that I was being filled by something else. The water was silky on my face, my arms and my legs. I envisioned it greening me, making me full, a mystery fern back from the dead, its desiccated fronds unfurling and filled with life.

ON MY WALK HOME FROM THE POOL, I stopped by the internet café. Fernando's email was brief and mysterious, instructing me, in Spanish, to wire a thousand pesos to a bank account in Mexico City and wait for instructions about a pickup location in Oaxaca City on an unnamed Thursday later that month. The fair lasted three days, Fernando wrote. There was no mention of where we were going or what would happen once we were there.

I was gambling again, a bit, but for a vision of a future that I wanted to invent. But now the uncertainty felt alluring, if not entirely safe. I wired the money and bought a plane ticket to Oaxaca City from Huatulco. Fuck it, I thought. Maybe I'll see some ferns yet.

CHAPTER 31 \\\\

THE NEXT SATURDAY, we were at the alitas bar again. The best alitas in town; the only alitas in town. The couple from Monterrey had decorated the second floor of the bar. Fairy lights hung over a few picnic tables painted in beachy pastels. I sat in a rope swing they'd installed near the railing, watching the night come alive below. Avenida Principal was frenetic with pink neon light, disco balls. Reggaeton clawed its way from several huge speakers up and down the street. Tourists in cowboy hats and airbrushed shirts meandered around the narrow dirt road, drinking cocktails out of Solo cups and wailing, hanging off one another.

A tall white guy in a T-shirt and tech shorts and a woman with long brown hair picked their way through the crowd, conspicuously sober. They were discussing something intensely—

the man was pointing out shops along the road as they walked. He turned his face in my direction and recognition shot through me. It was Carl, my brother's best friend from the Navy, the vegetarian who looked like Leonardo DiCaprio. But it couldn't be—it had been more than a decade since I'd seen him last. I had been so young then, too, a teenager, maybe late high school.

I slipped out of the swing and leaned over the banister on my elbows to study him better. There were wrinkles around his eyes, the skin soft around his jaw. I squinted. It was just another ghost, I thought. I remembered my brother at the coffee shop in New York so long ago. How he'd been a mentally ill guy instead. Well, a different mentally ill guy.

"Carl!" I shouted, before I could think about it. The man turned and cocked his head, bemused, for a moment. Then he smiled and waved. "Oh, hey!" he said, as if we'd bumped into each other at work. "What are you doing here?" I shouted, now fully disoriented. "Stay there," he said. "We'll be right up."

Except for my brother's stories, I'd only ever encountered Carl as my brother's little sister when they were stationed at a base in Honolulu, where my family had had lunch with them more than a decade ago. The sailors had been dressed in Hawaiian shirts and were enthusiastic only about surfing, the beaches, and the mischief available when they weren't working. I remember thinking they were so cool. After the military, my brother told me that Carl had become a photographer.

Carl strode across the roof deck, teeth flashing in the fairy lights, and gave me a hug. We had a drink, chatted about Mazunte. I realized that Carl and his friend perceived me as anyone else would, independent of my brother and my family. I was of the little world they'd found me in.

Carl explained he had spent a summer as a teenager living in Mazunte. He'd come back and found that everything was exactly how he'd remembered it. "Time moves differently here," he said. "No kidding," I said, laughing nervously, still awestruck at the coincidence, studying his face and his hands, thinking of how much had occurred since I last saw him. I wondered if he'd been in touch with my brother, if he knew what had happened. But I felt I couldn't ask.

"So what are *you* doing in Mazunte?" he asked me.

"Oh, I guess I'm here writing about ferns," I said, a little strained. I wanted him to think that I was a person with weight and direction, not someone's kid sister. "I'm a journalist," I added. As soon as the word left my mouth, I realized how insecure I sounded. How much it must have seemed like I was trying to convince myself of the thing I was telling them. I fiddled with my beer bottle, wondering if I should admit that I had no idea what I was doing in Mazunte, that my life had come undone and I mostly drank beer and came up with new ways of describing the ocean.

Carl pulled out his phone and used his thumbs to enlarge something on the screen. "Ferns, huh?" he said. He turned the screen around to show me, and I took it in my hands. It was an image of a wood fern in a forest, shot in panorama so that the fronds formed a wreath.

"I just took that yesterday," he said. "In the mountains, on the way down here. It's definitely the right time. The ferns there are huge right now—I mean, *gigantic*." I gave him his phone back and smiled, feeling shy and disoriented. "You gotta get out there, girl!" he said, putting the phone away.

I explained what I knew about the mysterious fair to him, expressed my worries about all the variables and ways that I assumed things might go wrong. How stupid I felt to not know any Spanish, to be hunting ferns alone in Mexico. He smiled warmly. "Sounds like an adventure," he said.

He finished his drink and glanced apologetically at his friend. "It was great to see you," he told me, his eyes sincere.

I felt regretful watching him get up; I wished I had been courageous enough to ask him about my brother, to explain why I was really in Mazunte. But I was frozen, unwilling to disrupt the magic of the coincidence, the niceness of the meeting. It had been enough to just have experienced it, perhaps, to experience a tangential confirmation of my brother's life and past. Carl turned at the stairs.

"Oh, hey," he said, walking back. "I'm going on that boat tour tomorrow morning that they advertise down by the main beach. It leaves right at sunrise. It's, like, fifty pesos. You should come."

I ARRIVED AT THE BEACH at dawn, the sun just beginning to peek above the sea. I sat on a dune, digging my feet into the night-cool sand. Young people hovered around, bearing white paper cups of coffee as boatmen in baseball caps and greasy tank tops fussed over half a dozen flat-bottomed boats that had been painted with wide stripes of bright color: vermilion, ultramarine, lemon yellow.

Carl arrived just as the men started pushing the skiffs into the ocean. He goofed around with me while we waited. We tied puffy orange life vests around our necks, and he showed me how to smear the lens of my phone camera with my finger to turn the sunrise into a four-pointed star. When the boatmen tried to split us into different boats, he negotiated with them jovially and instructed me to stick close by. We'd sit together no matter what, he told me. I was quiet, taking it all in as he entertained me and the others in the skiff with stories of traveling the world to take photographs, hiring teenagers in different countries to teach him to speak new languages over Skype. He had recently started Russian.

The skiff nosed its way out of the bay and into the sea, where the water grew choppy. The salt stung my skin. The sky turned from hazy pink to the clear blue light of day, and Carl motioned for me to hang off the railing of the boat so he could take a picture of me in the foreground of the sea. The boat wound its way around the natural rock formations along the coastline—Punta Ventanilla, with its picture window; Roca Blanca, white from guano. Pods of dolphins rode the current, and a manta ray flipped, glittering, into the air. Later, the skipper pointed into the distance and cranked the engine until we were riding so fast that the boat bounced on the water. He cut the engine just as suddenly and urged us all to look to the left of the skiff, where two massive flat forms cut through the sea.

"Humpback whales," Carl whispered to me, and the skipper puttered quietly toward them so that, for a few moments, they were gliding a city block away from us. It was calf riding with a mother, their cornflower-blue skin like satin. I don't think I breathed the entire time watching them, attempting to imagine the rest of their bodies from just this brief glimpse of skin. There was so much left unseen.

"Hey, so, what's the deal with your brother?" Carl asked me when the whales were gone and the skipper began turning us back to shore, the pace of the skiff mellow enough now to feel the sun on my back. The way he said it made me realize he'd been waiting to ask. "How is he? Do you know?" he asked. He explained that he hadn't heard from him in a while, longer than he and my brother usually went without speaking.

My stomach felt light. I'd spent the entire boat ride imagining what it would be like to speak to Carl frankly about my brother. I thought he might tell me something I didn't know, help me understand what had happened. My pulse quickened, and I felt overwhelmed attempting to fit the pieces together in my mind so that I might answer him. My eyes felt hot and damp. "I don't know, actually," I said. "I haven't seen him in years." It was all I could manage, even though it wasn't true. The last time I'd seen him was at the magazine, in the midst of a psychotic break. I just didn't know where to start. I looked back at the land, which was growing closer.

"You know, I called your parents' house a while ago to see if I could talk to Kang, and your dad answered," Carl said. I looked at him. He laughed wryly and looked down and then toward land. "He said he wasn't home and got kind of mad. He said never to call that number again." I wanted to apologize on behalf of Dad but found myself without words, reflecting on what had happened. The past few years must have been chaotic for my parents in a way I scarcely appreciated, my brother entirely at large, all of us crushed and confused by our shared and deteriorating world. An acknowledgment of those days from someone else outside my family lent a sudden clarifying reality to the situation. Jesus Christ, Kang was just out there, with military clearance, doing whatever the CIA in his head told him to, for years. Carl had sensed this, even if he couldn't have known what was on the other end of the receiver. He had been there too.

"You know, I have a brother who I never got along with very well," Carl said. "He's like, uh, a jock, I guess?" He trailed off. "Anyway, my mother got really sick recently and I went home for the first time in a while, and we were all together for the first time again. I wouldn't say we bonded, but . . . I did go to the gym with him." He smiled. I looked at him and smiled too. It felt generous, sharing as a form of care. A modicum of comfort offered without needing or expecting to know the specific dimension of my pain.

"I think about those Navy days with your brother all the time, actually," he said softly. "We were always trying to, like, fake injuries and stuff in Hawaii so that we could get out of our morning exercises and make it to class on time." They were taking classes at the University of Hawaii, I remembered. I imagined them, barely in their twenties, sneaking around so they could go out drinking all night, planning clandestine trips, shiny futures. "We were always late, running out of the showers and into the street half-dressed, trying to make it to the bus stop in time," he said, laughing and wiping his brow.

He fell silent then, the shore near enough that I could make out figures on the beach. I reflected on this memory, contained within Carl for so long. The feeling of it overlapped with the brother of my youth. I saw him then, and probably always will, as adventurous and free. He is still here, I kept thinking. He's here with us both.

Then we were jumping into the water. The skipper needed us off so he could dock. The sun filtered through the salt water and touched the backs of my hands, and the colors and shapes on the shore slowly blew into form.

LATER THAT WEEK, I sat on a small skiff on a brackish lagoon under a deep violet sky hung with stars. The trees lining the shore creaked in the wind, their silhouetted branches against the sky like a shadow screen. Adriana had driven the welder, brave Mateo, and me here on a lark. We were an hour or so outside Mazunte. She wanted me to swim in the lagoon before I left for Oaxaca City the following morning.

Through a series of exchanges with Fernando in broken Spanish, I'd worked out that the plant fair occurred somewhere outside Oaxaca City. Fernando suggested that I pack a rain jacket for the trip—we were slowly coming into wet season. In Oaxaca City, I would meet a white van outside the baseball stadium at 5:00 a.m. on Saturday. Adriana was predictably thrilled I had decided to go.

I peered out onto the dark water, moonlight glinting off the ripples from the boat. Around us was more frog music, owls in the distance. When we arrived in the middle of the lagoon, the driver extinguished his lantern, and the darkness was leavened only by the stars.

"Now you can swim," Adriana said, pointing to the black water. "Not me. I just watch," she clarified. I moved gingerly to the back of the skiff. There were only different shades of black, and my imagination conjured shifting forms in the water. I looked back at Adriana. "I just dive in?" I asked her dumbly. The welder and the others in our boat were stripping their clothes off. Mateo peered over the edge of the hull into the water, dipping his hand in tentatively. Adri nodded.

I took a deep breath, pressed my arms and hands into an arrow above my head, and dove into the water. It was frigid. The air licked my face when I surfaced. I opened my eyes and saw the outline of my legs in tiny, crackling lights. My hands were covered in tiny splinters of light, as if I'd punched through a square of sunlight on the floor. I had no idea what I was looking at. I splashed my hands directly in front of my eyes. The water coruscated, bioluminescence sparkling from every drop. I swam furiously in all directions around the boat, kicking the water into the air to see how bright it would become, to try to extend the light for as long as I could.

My fear of the darkness and the depths of the lagoon faded as I played, diving down into the blackness to see just how far the bioluminescence reached. I rolled onto my back again, floating, and clapped the water just in front of my nose, wanting to come as close to the light as I could. It's real, I kept thinking to myself, even though it felt like I was the only one to see it. It was real, this fire around the edges of the air. It was all real.

CHAPTER 32 \\\\

A FEW DAYS LATER, I sat on the curb of a McDonald's on the outskirts of Oaxaca City in the pitch-black morning, pulling a wool shirt I'd bought at a street stand tighter. The streetlights were sodium-vapor orange on the asphalt. Cars and trucks thundered by on the nearby overpass. I kept looking at my phone. It was 5:30, then 5:45. I kept checking my email to make sure I'd gotten the directions right. Yes, it was the right day. Yes, it was the right time. I could see the baseball stadium from where I was sitting.

At six, I began to wonder if they'd left without me and started contemplating what I might do with the rest of my week-end. I was frustrated with myself, but a little relieved. Maybe it was better for the whole thing to fall through. I was rehearsing what I'd say to Adriana about it when a white minivan pulled up in front of me. A woman with a clipboard stepped out and started speaking to me in rapid and attentive Spanish. I tried my best to respond, pulling up Fernando's email on my phone. She waved me into the vehicle, and I found an empty seat in the middle row. The five or six passengers were all sleeping peacefully, their gentle snores filling the cab. I dropped my backpack into the aisle, and we pulled away.

I WOKE UP A FEW HOURS LATER to a martian landscape: flat red clay punctuated now and then by enormous cacti or agave bursting into towering staffs of yellow flowers. The sky was cyan. Why were we still driving? I wondered sleepily, startled to still be on the road. I had assumed that the trip would take an hour or two. Some of the passengers had started to wake up and were speaking to one another softly in Spanish. I tried not to panic, realizing I had no idea where I was or where we were going. The children in the back seat were teasing each other, and their mother kept shushing them. I stared out the window as the landscape transformed and our route grew windy, the little van rocking back and forth.

The red landscape dried up into beige desert hills inlaid with dusty paths. They rose irregularly, ziggurats ornamented by scraggly brush, and as we wound around them higher and higher, one side of the highway gave way to an enormous cliff. In the distance, an olive mountain range was shrouded in smoke. *Tienditas* selling ceramics and crafts dotted the road, and every now and then a Chinese buffet or a produce stand appeared. We seemed to descend, and the landscape changed again into dense pine forest, the edges of the asphalt furred with drifts of orange needles. The temperature dropped quickly.

I was still in cutoff shorts and a sports bra. All I had known of Oaxaca to this point was the unrelenting heat. I clutched the wool shirt around me now as tightly as I could. I felt a tap on my shoulder, and when I turned around, the woman sitting next to me was awake and holding out a tasseled black scarf to me. She smiled encouragingly. She looked like she was in her fifties, with a kind, round face and an auburn bob.

I thanked her effusively and wrapped the scarf around my thighs. I smiled at her sheepishly, rubbing my hands together. She furrowed her brow and began listing off the names of various languages. "*Français?*" she asked. "*Deutsche?*" I shook my head apologetically, heart sinking as she went down the list. A bit humiliated, I thought back to my friends in Mazunte, how content my mute life had been on the coast.

"*Ingles?*" she finally asked, and I nodded and laughed from relief, almost crying. She introduced herself as Elvira. "It gets very cold in the mountains," she said, smiling warmly. "We are at the very top now, and to arrive at the cloud forest we'll have to go down a little bit. It won't be as cold there." My mind lingered on the words *cloud forest*. Very literary, I thought, imagining something ethereal, a palace in the sky. Elvira asked me how I'd found myself here. I confessed everything—how I didn't speak Spanish, how I didn't really know what the fair was, even. I told her I was a journalist who was interested in helechos, trotting out one of the only Spanish words I felt confident about.

"Ah," she said, pausing for a moment to think. "There are many helechos where we are going." She smiled and told me that she was a biological ecologist and interested in the Indigenous communities who lived deep in the mountains. Society posed a dilemma for their villages—how much modernity should they let in? Electricity, plumbing? How much of their own cultures could be preserved? The area we were going to was named La Chinantla, she told me. A word that meant "an enclosed space" in Aztec, an acknowledgment of how difficult the region is to access.

She was interested in the stories the villagers told, what responsibility academics were meant to take in the ongoing formation of their stories. "Take python, for example," she said. Oh shit. "Wait," I said. "Like the big snake?" Where were we going?

"Yes," Elvira said drily, "like the big snake. Once, long ago, there was a python that went into someone's house and ate a baby."

"It ate a baby?" I repeated.

"Sí, yes, a baby," she said patiently. "And I am sure that this happened, the python eating a baby. But it must have been a very long time ago. Yet still the Chinantec people keep this story with them, and even now, whenever they see python, they cut off its head, no matter where they are." I imagined a ravine filled with the headless bodies of gigantic snakes.

"But python are basically not dangerous to people, not normally. And they are becoming quite endangered." She paused, looking out the window, where the landscape was growing lusher and emerald, slick with dew. I loosened the scarf. "So we tried to work with them to tell them to stop killing pythons, and convince them to trust us because we are scientists," she said. "But it's hard because it is their story and part of their culture." I contemplated this for a moment, the tension between what feels certain in the body and what is known in the mind. The strange competing territory that exists in a person.

"Or your helechos, for instance," she said. "There is one, called brake, that is invasive here." I nodded, thinking of bracken, their large leathery fronds, how they could tower above my head. "The natives believe that all plants have a spirit, that they are sacred. But these brakes overgrow everything—native species, crops. We can't seem to convince them that it is not a good plant to keep, that they should try to kill it when it grows," Elvira said, her words tinged with the frustration of her disregarded scientific evidence. I couldn't help but feel compassion for their reliance on story and emotion. I was that way too.

Little eruptions of fern were appearing along the road, tiny bursts of green floating just above the rocks in the exposed mountain. I was becoming very excited. I saw fern leaves as tall and as wide as a person draped over exposed mountain faces. We steered around treacherous passes, sharp corners, and steep inclines, my eyes tracking these fronds the whole time.

A fiddlehead whose stem was as thick as my forearm, covered in dense gold fur, emerged from a rock face. Its pinnae were in stages of unraveling, and a few were as big as flags, wavering in the wind. I pointed it out to Elvira. "What is that?" I asked. "Why is it so big?" She put on her glasses and squinted. "Oh, that. A tree fern. There are many here."

I had the same eerie feeling as when I'd spotted Carl in Mazunte just a few weeks earlier. Tree ferns. I had encountered them in my reading before I left Mazunte, but what I had learned about them made them seem mostly endangered, specimens carefully tended at botanical gardens, not exploding from the woods at every turn.

We turned a corner, and white smoke surrounded the van. Our driver slowed to a crawl. During a brief clearing, I saw what it was: white and billowing, out of place just above the ground. It was a cloud. We were in a cloud. I laughed out loud, understanding now that the name of the forest was literal. We nosed into another cloud, descending.

THE VAN UNLOADED US at a tiny folding table in a small clearing in a jungle shrouded in clouds. I slapped at my thighs and neck. Tiny black-and-white mosquitoes gifted me painful welts, each with a single point of blood at its center. Behind a flimsy white folding table, a tall man in his fifties with a jovial face was wearing a nametag that read *Fernando*. Fernando! He was checking people on the clipboard one by one, and when it was my turn, I tried to explain to him who I was, but he had no English. Elvira was somewhere else, and no one was able to translate. My phone had no service. We chatted at each other uselessly until he was struck with a realization. "Ahhhh, Wei," he said, nodding furiously in recognition. I watched him pencil in a checkmark on his spreadsheet next to the word *güey*. He handed me paper and pencil, and I was forlorn, scanning the Spanish on the page.

Elvira reappeared, explaining that the form listed activities. I should check the ones I wanted to participate in over the next three days. I asked her what I should want to do, and she looked at me with deep skepticism, hastily checked a few boxes, and handed the paper back to Fernando. I felt like a child, desperate to ask more but unwilling to swallow more humiliation.

Someone else urged me to get into the bed of a nearby truck with some others. Okay, fine, at least there was, uh, a railing welded to the bed. No English. I hoped that Elvira would join us, but she was still standing near Fernando when we pulled away. The forest swallowed them, and I began to panic very mildly. Is this how my mother felt, I thought, arriving in America without language? Shuttled here and there? We clung onto the railing—I should not have mocked it—as the truck careened up a winding mountain pass.

We stopped at a tiny village—really just six or seven houses and a cement basketball court—then another. The second held a cedar cabin built into the hill, lined with doors like a tiny motel. I mutely followed everyone to the cabin. A woman in

a navy blue shirt was wrangling two small children; I recognized her as one of the passengers in the van. She noticed
that I was watching her and sympathetically pointed to a door
next to the door she was opening. I followed her direction and
opened it. Inside was a long room lined by eight or ten metal
bunk beds. A single lightbulb hung from the ceiling.

I chose the bottom bunk next to the door, dropped my backpack, and sat on the thin mattress. My body was vibrating un-
pleasantly. I was again hungry and cold. I assumed that others would come eventually and fill the other beds, but no one
came. Instead, I sat there alone, in the half-light, for what felt
like hours, turning my phone on and off, staring at the screen,
compulsively opening and closing apps even though there was
no service. I wondered if anything would happen, poking my
head out the door every now and then in case the others were
leaving again to do something else. But they never did. What
was I supposed to eat? Was I supposed to stay put? What if
they forgot about me? Had they already?

I was furious at myself for vanity and idiocy, for getting myself into this mess. I was increasingly freezing and scared, and
the bathroom was a hole dug into the ground in a small wooden
structure nearby. I was also terribly embarrassed, knowing I
couldn't communicate myself to anyone around me. I angrily
thought about how in New York I was someone with friends
and a job and a modicum of security. And even if my family
was insane enough to write a small book about, they existed.
Now I was completely alone, like I'd wanted. What, I thought
I could just leave my life and be okay? Pride, arrogance, self-
pity, shame at all the above. I wiped my face with the blanket,
watching my bulb sway slightly, hearing the footfalls of the
others in their rooms in the cabin. The pangs in my chest were
relentless. I got under the thin blanket, close to crying.

I was in the middle of another round of deep breaths when I noticed a second door on the far end of the room. I took a paperback copy of Oliver Sacks's *Oaxaca Journal* as a totem and crossed the room. I opened the door and stepped onto an enormous back porch that overlooked the great valleys and mountains of the cloud forest. My ravening interior world disappeared. I leaned over the banister and took in the undulating jade ridge, the white mist dense in some places and gauzy in others. There were a few others on the porch, sitting and chatting. There were children playing cards on the floor. I sat in a wicker chair nearby and began to read.

Eventually, I noticed the woman in the navy blue shirt who had helped me locate my room and put down my book to go speak with her. "*Muchos gracias por ayudar,*" I said inexpertly and attempted to seem as if I hadn't just been crying and staring at a lightbulb. She smiled and nodded. A little boy ran up and wrapped himself around her leg, peering up at me.

"Um," I announced. "*Yo no entiendo español.*" I eloquently thrashed my hands at our surroundings, at the others on the porch, and shook my head furiously. My eyes grew hot. She smiled steadily and answered in a soft, patient stream of Spanish, tapping her index finger in her palm as she explained what I guessed had been the events of the day, the situation at the cabin, the make of the cosmos. She asked me a question. I recognized the word *rio*, so I nodded, more in recognition than assent. "Okay!" she said, and then pointed at herself and then at her room. Then she pointed at my room and walked up to it and gestured knocking at the door. "Okay!" I said, confident that there was a plan and it involved doors.

In my room, I changed optimistically into a bathing suit and fiddled with my disconnected phone until I heard a rap at my door. I followed my new friend, whose name was Leah, and her two children down the steps of the cabin and down a small hill, where there was a damp stone staircase. We picked our way down it and along a shaded trail until we came to a clearing through which there was a river that the children sprinted toward, throwing their shirts off and diving into the water.

Leah and I made it to the shore of the river at a slower pace. The gray day swam on the surface of the water, which appeared green, though it was clear. The jungle on the other side of the bank remained dark and forbidding. She pointed at me, made paddling motions with her hands, then pointed to the water. I stepped into the icy river, and goose bumps rose on my thighs. I climbed onto a huge boulder in the middle of the river and watched as the children collected rocks to show Leah. I waved at her and smiled when she looked at me, wanting her to believe I was content, that I waded tentatively into freezing rivers all the time at home.

I had rarely felt so alone. And yet, my inner world was shimmering with activity. Inside of me grew an expanse of sadness, of confusion, of anger—at myself, at the fair, at where I was in my life more generally. The natural world around me was dense and impenetrable and close. I'd gone to the ferns. But it felt unbearable and was dislocated from it, insulated by worry. If only someone else were here who might translate the experience for me, I kept thinking. If only someone would tell me where to look or how to be. Me as me, there was no way of making these woods coherent. What had memorizing the genera of fern prepared me for, exactly? What had I thought that would be useful for?

A streak of red flashed past, low over the water, and landed on my rock, scarlet wings opening and closing slowly. The butterfly flattened itself out against the stone, and I saw that its forewings were striped like a zebra and its hind wings were decorated by four white circles arranged like the number *88*. Was I seeing that correctly? I watched it launch itself again into the wind, blinking its way upstream, disappearing around a bend.

I ACCEPTED MY MUTENESS. There wasn't another option. Everyone at the fair seemed to know that I was wandering around like a toddler, so someone would come gather me for meals or a ride in the flatbed truck to a lecture about the agricultural strategy known as a milpa given on the basketball court. One evening after dinner, there was a slideshow of night-vision images of toucans and a video of a jaguar smacking around a boar twice its size. Clearly, someone had allowed the scientists cameras in the woods. Afterward we ate grilled corn slathered in mayonnaise and Tajín.

I was confused most of the time, but I came to understand that the fair was about Chinantlan culture. I appreciated its broad, scrappy range of programming, maybe especially because I could experience it only with my senses. But I was still at the mercy of everyone around me when it came to whens and wheres. Once, after a children's dance show, I was given a calabash bowl of honey, chile peppers, bananas, and soap, all farmed and produced in the jungle, and after spending a full ten minutes in feelings of confusion and anxiety, unsure of whether the products were a gift or what, I looked up and realized I'd lost my group.

I sat on the edge of a basketball court alone for two hours, wondering if anyone would come find me. Without language, my other senses expanded. I took in everything around me: the smell of rain falling into dirt, Inca doves calling from a distance, small children banded together around a basketball.

Eventually I arrived at a version of joy, reflecting on how stupid I could be, how it was okay and even a little pleasurable to sit on a cement basketball court with a basket of soap. I stopped caring so much about how others might perceive me. It was obvious, for one, that I was out of place—I was the only Asian, the only American, the only one who couldn't speak any Spanish, the only one wearing the same dirty sweat pants every day.

By the third day, I felt relaxed by the melodic patter at the breakfast table. It was as if I'd excused myself from language completely, happy to not be known or to know. I needed the intimacy of those around me, certainly, and I needed the sound of voices and the feeling of bodies. But every moment felt full without expression. I knew that Leah and the kids would look forward to seeing me when I woke up. I knew there would be some strange and unpredictable adventure in the afternoon. I knew to look forward to the yuca tortillas the kitchen served each morning—they were thick and chewy like mochi, a little charred from the comal. I ripped them into pieces like others at the table and rolled them up into fat cigars to scoop up black beans from my plate.

After breakfast, I was told to go to the river. When I arrived, there were half a dozen Chinantlans gathering river rocks around a bonfire on the banks of the river. I sat on a rock and watched them pile the stones onto the charred wood. When it started to rain, they set up a red tarp by the fire for all of us to stand underneath. It cast a purple glow over everyone's faces as they worked. Later, women in dresses embroidered with colorful flowers brought plastic buckets of tomatoes, onions, cilantro, and small, chubby fish and began preparing them. By the river, the rain fell into an embankment of ferns. I hadn't noticed them before. They were enormous, I thought, and so beautiful.

I wandered over to them, pushing the blades apart with my hands to study their handkerchief fronds; the tips draped over in a tidal curl. They were silky on my fingers; there were sori shaped like plates on the backs of their pinnae, their indusia lightly attached. Another fern nearby seemed identical to this one, until I looked closer and noticed that its sori were like eyelids in rows. Nearby, there was a cascade of maidenhairs on a boulder near the river. Its pinnae were kelly green and a delicate peach; tiny spheres of water accumulated on its scalloped edges. I was getting soaked in the rain, but I didn't care. I noticed now that the stone wall near the staircase was busy with tiny plants. Just a few days ago, when I passed it to go to the river, it had been unremarkable. Or had my despair been too great for me to notice? But now I saw that the entire face was covered by a riot of ferns and spike mosses weaving in and out of one another in shades of green, purple, and pink. They glistened like a tide pool as rain trickled over the wall.

Some Chinantlans emerged at the top of the staircase, hauling something wooden and enormous and plastic-covered on their shoulders. I wandered back under the tarp to give them space. It looked like a piece of furniture—a console or a dresser—and the sides were intricately carved with flowers. They set it down under the tarp and removed the plastic, and a man pulled out two mallets and began to lightly tap on the top. Spooky hollow notes. A marimba. He practiced scales quietly, before launching into a song I didn't recognize. By then, familiar faces were filing down the staircase—Leah and her kids, Fernando, Elvira, who waved at me from afar.

The Chinantlans were splitting tree branches at their ends with a hatchet and using them to rummage through the coals of the bonfire and pinch hot stones between the spliced wood. Nearby, women were filling each calabash bowl with chopped cilantro, onion, and tomatoes, bottled water, and a single fish, and lining them up on a bench. The men dropped red-hot stones into each bowl, setting a furious boil into the water. When the stones cooled, they were returned into the fire. A woman handed me a bowl of the fish soup with a large wooden spoon.

I gathered a little bit of everything in the soup into my spoon, anticipating something delicious. All weekend, I'd been spoiled by the orange and red moles and the unique tubers and palm flowers of jungle cuisine. But a mouthful of the broth tasted like dirt and watered-down tomatoes. Grit from the rocks crunched between my teeth. I grimaced, feeling the instinct to spit it out. But Elvira caught my attention from the other side of the tent. She raised her spoon at me, and I swallowed hard and tried my best to smile back. The marimba player was playing "Guantanamera." I glanced again at the ferns on the riverbank glittering in the rain. I was at peace.

THE NEXT MORNING, Leah woke me up, knocking on my door before sunrise. She spoke to me in an urgent stream of Spanish in which the word *helecho* kept appearing. Knowing how these things went, I put on my raincoat and sneakers and waited in front of the cabin with our little group. A short man in a baseball cap, carrying a machete, arrived as light began to seep into the sky. He moved at a fast clip.

I trailed behind the rest of the group as we passed through farmland, then dry forest, then jungle, stopping to investigate the many and astonishing ferns. There were iridescent blue ferns in the shape of clover, rising up on tall spindly stems. There were ferns shaped like talons padding around a mossy thin tree, their sori distributed like a scatterplot on the backs of their pinnae. In the deep woods, near bromeliads the size of golf carts, there were bird's-nest ferns perched on fallen trees, their waxy crowns glowing like phosphor. The rock faces of the trail dripped with spike mosses like a tangle of ribbons, their pinnae flares of green fire.

In a low-lying stream, where the air felt both humid and cold, I spotted something purplish and translucent wedged under a boulder. Feeling bold, I tucked it into my pocket. Later when we arrived at a sunny clearing, I pulled the leaf out and laid it on my hand. It was a filmy fern, translucent emerald and fuchsia. I could see the lines of my palm through the leaf. I twirled it in the air to see how the sun filtered dreamlike through its gauzy tissue. Dark purple veins fissured to rippled edges, which contained miniature cones full of sori. I thought of the Solutrean chert knives Annie Dillard once described, knapped so thin that the blades thinned "from transparency to transparency"; I thought of how they were never meant to be used. Their existence attested to the fact that "someone thought of making, and made, this difficult, impossible, beautiful thing." The filmy fern dried out in seconds in the clearing and I felt moved and at once melancholy. When it was time to set off again, it had shriveled to a flake of green.

The light was clearer as we ascended a gradual incline. I assumed we were drawing closer to the canopy. Sunbeams on the jungle floor found plush, dense yellow-green mosses. I kept getting distracted by ferns, overwhelmed now by groves of glossy, zigzagging pinnules, of fiddleheads hanging heavy like dew from horizontal stems. I hung behind to touch them, to observe their sori and eventually realized that my group had turned a corner in the distance without me. When I caught up, everyone was silent, their eyes fixed beyond the path, which had given way to a deep, mist-filled valley.

A grove of enormous spindly trees lay before us. The trunks were strangely furred, and the light fell into fragments, making dense bright patchwork on their boles and branches. I traced the trunk of a single specimen upward, ninety, a hundred feet, to a lacy green parasol. At its center, there was a clutch of tightly wound croziers. I was barely breathing.

To see tree ferns is to experience deep time. I was acutely aware of my body, of my breathing, of how everything around me was fern. I was as close as a person could get, reaching my hand out to rest it on a trunk, no story in my mind except for the feeling of the damp bark against my skin, the leaves overhead. The light as it found us through the lace of the fronds.

An inarticulable question accompanied me in the cloud forest and came to visit now in that silence, something to do with ferns and who I was and why anyone would write a book that is half fern and half family. Here was the answer, as simple and inarticulable as the question: the feeling of wholeness, knowing that this place stood as it did and had always been so. I wandered over to a young tree fern near the path. It was only as tall as my hip. At its center two fiddleheads in golden fur, each stem as thick as my forearm. I skimmed my hand over the center of one crozier, tracing my fingertips first around its coil then over its tightly packed leaves. They were just beginning to unravel.

CHAPTER 33 \\\\

I FOUND ENGLISH IN the cloud forest eventually, but not until the end. Two women about my age asked me if I spoke English—I'd only ever heard them chatting in Spanish. When I nodded, they immediately broke out into the language, apologizing to me for not knowing sooner and helping me. One of the girls, Iliana, was Mexican; the other, Diana, was an American who worked with people in small villages around Oaxaca. Iliana was fair and lithe and dark-haired. Diana was blond and woodsy. Both lived in Oaxaca City and had met Fernando like I had—a friend of a friend, a receipt at a bar. They told me he was, through his networks of friends and converts, always persuading everyone to come see what it was like here. We got along easily.

The girls invited me to come stay in their cabin for the last night of the fair. It was just down the hill from the cabin I had been staying in, but it was a modern structure, with running water, a working toilet, walls, and insulation. There were locks on the doors. I almost laughed walking into it. Hot water, a ceramic toilet. It felt luxurious. I was drunk that evening on English, listening greedily as Diana and Iliana explained the interpersonal dynamics of the attendees of the cloud forest. They told me that the villagers were hoping to build ecotourism infrastructure in La Chinantla to make money and to preserve the deep forest, which was quickly being destroyed by logging, ranching, and agriculture.

The next morning, the sun was out for the first time since we'd arrived. The girls told me that normally it was so sunny the weekend of the fair that most of the attendees spent the entire weekend in the river.

Over a breakfast of yuca tortillas and eggs fried in licorice-scented hoja santa leaves, I asked Diana how she'd managed to become fluent in Spanish. Her language was soft, with a lilting accent, free of the flat, dead vowels in U.S.-accented Spanish. I was surprised to learn she was from the United States. A mischievous expression washed over the face of Iliana, who was sitting beside her. She answered on Diana's behalf: "You move in with your Colombian boyfriend."

Diana laughed and tore her tortilla into pieces. "You know, I think for me learning languages has always followed a similar trajectory. When you're first learning, you feel helpless." She swallowed a piece of tortilla, sipped her coffee. "Then, at some point, you move from that stage to feeling like you're an impostor. Everything you say is pretend, and everyone knows it. Eventually, you move on from that too, and you begin to relax into it and you become yourself. It happens without you noticing, I think." She looked back at Iliana. "I don't think you're fluent until you start having a sense of humor in the language, really. It's like getting a new personality or something."

Iliana nodded. "In Spanish, I think you are a little more soft-spoken, no?" she said, furrowing her brow. "In English, you seem much more serious, but also funnier. We talk more about intellectual things." Diana laughed.

"Oh, so you think I sound cute and dumb in Spanish!" Diana said. "I don't know as many words in Spanish. Anyway, I'm learning Portuguese right now too. In that language, I'm at the impostor phase," she said. "Wei, what about you? Do you speak other languages?"

I said that I spoke Shanghainese. "It's close to Mandarin. But it sounds a lot softer," I said. "And the humor is a lot more macabre." They laughed.

"Do you feel like you can be yourself in Shanghainese?" Iliana asked. I paused. It was a question I hadn't considered before. I didn't have an answer prepared..

"Well," I said, "it was the language I spoke with my family at home. It's actually my first language. And I don't know if you know this, but in Chinese culture there's a lot of really rigid hierarchies about people being older and having more power or younger and less. So, for instance, I was never allowed to call my older brother by his first name. I got hit for that kind of thing, actually." (Iliana mouthed the word *wow*.) "Anyway, I guess in my head, that means that in Shanghainese, I'm a version of myself that is still in my family's home. So, like, I'm the baby, and the only girl, and the only one who didn't grow up in China, so I really had to listen to everyone around me and watch them to try to understand how I was supposed to be in this family or out in the world.

"And gosh, on top of that there were just so many expectations. Like, I mean, they wanted my brother to be a doctor so bad that I think he kind of went nuts? I mean that literally, he actually has paranoid schizophrenia. I was there, it sucked. And that took the pressure off of me, in a lot of ways. Also I'm a girl, so the stakes just aren't as high, because it's not like I can pass on the family name." I looked down at my plate, at the remaining half of my yuca tortilla. Diana and Iliana waited.

"What I mean is that in China, after you get married, you don't belong to your original family anymore. You belong to your husband's family. At least that's how my parents feel about it, so if I don't become a doctor, it's not necessarily their problem, I guess. There was a lot of pressure to, like, go to an Ivy League school, or to marry someone really impressive and have lots of kids, or to just get a normal good-ass job. I don't think anyone ever really believed I could become a writer or a journalist, and even now that I am pretty much a working journalist, I know they're proud of me in certain ways, but I don't think that it's the story they wanted." Behind their heads I could make out the shape of the mountains, the clear sky startling blue. The forest was emerald today, the sun moving over it in planes of light. "What I wanted was to be loved by everyone, to just be like them, to be one of the family, like when I was little and all that mattered was being there. That just always makes me feel so small in all of these ways, so tiny. I guess the person I am in Shanghainese is someone who is very little, like a daughter, or like a little seed that's just blowing around."

CHAPTER 34 \\\\

AFTER BREAKFAST, ILIANA INVITED ME to walk to the next village, where we would meet Diana and the truck back to Oaxaca City. She told me that the villagers walked this trail. The trucks were here for the fair. We gave our bags to the others, and set off with the same guide who had taken us through the forest to see the tree ferns the day before. His name was Don Pedro, and Iliana and Diana told me that they called him the forest sage—he knew everything about La Chinantla. He had been raised in the jungle. When he was young, he had served as a guide for the zoologists and botanists who came to study the cloud forest. From them he'd learned the scientific names of the cloud forest's plants and animals. Along the route, he showed us where his home was. There were many banana trees planted out front; each produced a different kind of banana. He gave each of us a fat purple one to eat as we walked.

"I was thinking about what you were saying earlier, about being Chinese or not," Iliana said to me. "You know, I'm Jewish; I don't look Mexicana. I look white. I never really thought about it like that," she continued. "My family, lots of them, are from the Caribbean. Some of them look like me, some of them don't. My accent in English changes depending on who I'm around, and I have all these Jamaican relatives. When I get around them, I start to speak like this, mon." She laughed. "I can't help it," she said, picking a flower from a bush and looking at it.

"I *feel* Mexicana," she said, tapping the flower against her palm. "As Mexican as anyone, even if people don't think I look like it. Even my name, *Iliana*. That's a very Mexican name." We were both starting to sweat, and she paused to wipe her brow. Our guide looked back at us. The forest had a different mood this morning, bright green and translucent, pink and purple with flowers. Birds and insects made brief streaks of color between trees.

"You know, sometimes they call Asian Americans like me 'bananas,'" I said, and we both laughed, she after an appropriate beat.

"Actually, I'm remembering now that they say that maybe the Chinantec people have Chinese blood," Iliana said. "Maybe you are cousins with Don Pedro."

"Really?" I said. "Chinese blood. Why do they think that?" Iliana shrugged and opened a line of questioning with Pedro. Two questions in, he stopped walking and became effusive, glancing at me now and then and waving his hands. He set off walking again in a different direction, on a path that went steeply uphill. We followed.

"What'd he say?" I asked Iliana, just catching up, short of breath.

"Oh, he said it's something from long ago, he doesn't really know the details," she said. "But sometimes in the village there are children who are born who look Chinese." We came across a clearing where there sat a simple one-story building, white with floor-to-ceiling windows. Light slanted across it. It looked strangely modern, even suburban, perched on a freshly mowed lawn, jungle behind it. Iliana explained that it was the combined school for the two villages. Don Pedro motioned for us to wait and jogged through the front door.

A few minutes later he dragged out a mussy-haired teenager in a striped blue T-shirt. When they got closer to us, Don Pedro let go of the boy, fired off some Spanish, and pointed at me.

Don Pedro made eye contact with me then and grabbed the boy's forearm, pointed to it, then pointed to my forearm, speaking to the boy in Nahuatl. He pointed to the boy's eyes, then pointed at mine. It was a farce, yes, but in a literal sense Don Pedro wasn't wrong. This boy's skin was golden, the undertone turmeric, a lot like mine. And his eyes were almond shaped. I could've been his cousin. I started laughing, and Don Pedro and Iliana were laughing too. Don Pedro patted the boy on the shoulder. The teenager took a shy look at me, us in our race of two, then loped away. The rest of us were left grinning at each other, locked into this ad hoc conspiracy, here, in the middle of everything, in the cloud forest of Oaxaca.

DEEP IN LA CHINANTLA, there are seven lagoons—crystal clear with trees growing eerily in the middle of them. (In my imagination they are aquamarine as swimming pools, each glowing, the buttressed roots of the trees gnarled and black.)

The lagoons are enchanted, and you are forbidden to swim in them. If the water is touched by human hands, it will rain. ("That doesn't seem so bad," I whisper to Diana, who is translating as Fernando tells these stories. "It already seems to rain a lot here?" I say, hoping she'll clarify the point about the rain. She waves me off so she can keep listening.) The villagers who live nearby the lagoons gather water using cups and spoons.

In another part of the forest, the day before the day of the dead, there is a monster. ("*El duende del bosque,*" Fernando whispers, eyes wide.) The duende can be seen at dusk, his head just above the canopy of the cloud forest. (I imagine the head a huge, moss-covered boulder with maidenhairs and tiny white flowers trailing over the eye sockets. Where its head skims the canopy, birds flee in black sparks.) Once, after some villagers collected an enormous pile of firewood around sunset for a holiday, the pile vanished by morning. All that was left were enormous footprints leading back into the bosque.

I feel afraid that the cloud forest will disappear one day soon and with it the lagoons, the duende, the chatter of birds high in the canopy. The limitless grove of tree ferns. Do ghost stories warn us to take better care of what we have? To remain humble in the face of nature and the unknown? Are they a reminder that whatever we have at any moment is enough? We tell ghost stories, I think, because our ghosts are real.

BACK IN MAZUNTE, I felt that I was ready to return to New York, to meet myself there again, whatever I had become. The day before my flight, I wrote a final letter to my brother's ghost, to the person I had been chasing my entire life.

I wrote to him about my thirtieth birthday party, a few months before, how I wished he'd been there. It had been four years since I had last seen him, and I said I was sorry for the many years that I hadn't called to wish him a happy birthday. I was only beginning to understand why and how I had made him into something that wasn't true, into something that had to protect me and, when it failed to protect me, that I could hate. But like a revolving door, our shared home, the magazine, the Spider all came back to me changed and rotated. It was a story I was getting braver at waking up into every day.

I thanked him for his care when I was small, told him I was grateful that he had lit a path for me to follow. Did he remember the time we took windsurfing gear out on the lake in Tennessee? I still remembered sitting on a board, floating on the still black water as he hoisted a multicolored sail into the air, catching and being borne aloft by some unseen current. I looked back now and could feel again how much he loved me. I knew he still did. The love I wanted was open and steady, so I had to learn to be too.

Brother, I miss you, I wrote. I knew it was time to let my fantasy of him go, to try to see what was really there.

The next morning, I folded up the letter to the person who didn't exist and walked the familiar path out to Punta Cometa. The limestone was on fire with morning sun, the waves white against the cliffs. I found a patch of dirt and dug a small hole and set the letter under a stone. I lit a match and touched it to the corner of a page. It smoldered, a bit stubborn. I wondered if the rest of the pages would catch, but a breath of wind came up and consumed the pages and carried the fine black ash over the waves.

EPILOGUE \\\\

IN MY MEMORY, SHANGHAI IS a dark place, the narrow longtongs, the dark, crowded apartments, the constant sound of shuffling, of voices in another room. I think of it as a passage to the underworld—my memories are of searching for graves or watching my grandmother grow frail or the funeral of my mother's younger brother, who died of an asthma attack the week we landed in 2002.

But Mama promises me that this time, when I visit with her and Baba, our only motive is to have fun. We don't tell any relatives we are going to be in town. This trip is for us.

Before we leave, I dream of celadon-green caterpillars. They spill out of picture frames, hang in the air, transform into dragons, paper, silks. I don't know what they mean. My therapist suggests that paper and silk are Chinese treasures. I reflect on this while I pack. I am starting to believe in something that still feels frightening and impossible—living only within each day, within each moment. Learning what pleasure feels like, learning how to like it. I have won these lessons and placed them at the center of my life with my own hands.

There is joy in Shanghai. It's autumn, and Mama and Baba and I are in good spirits, devouring dazha crabs where we can find them, pork mooncakes, Italian ice, haggling over shirts at the silk market, Nanjing Lu with its ancient linden trees. We visit Chenghuang Miao and light incense, buy kilos of tea. We follow the Huangpugong at night and marvel at the firework skyline of Pudong. Wherever we go, Mama and Baba point to buildings I'll never remember and tell me about a Shanghai long ago, forever unfolding in these high-rises, these schools, these offices. They float across the city, never asking for directions. The buildings have changed, groaning with the weight of cash and steel and a new world, but the layout is ancient. And I'm fluent here too, but in a new way. Shanghainese is no longer the language of my family, of four people trapped in a house in Tennessee; it's the language of the biggest city that humans have ever built.

We hire a car to Taicang, my father's ancestral home. He hasn't been there since he was a young man, younger than I am now. I watch as Shanghai retreats, leaving to us open fields and highway. I feel small again, but as if I am one of three children, playing together in a big world. Here and there, I'm able to see them apart from our relationship to each other as mother, father, and daughter. For reasons I can almost understand, Shanghai has broken us apart. My father, sitting to my left, is an elegant and charismatic doctor, entering his middle seventies, returning to a place he has last seen at twenty-six. My mother, gazing at endless fields of passing sorghum, is a musician, a composer who hears a windy and indescribable music in her dreams no has ever heard nor will ever hear again. A woman who worries about her son. I am in the car with them.

The smog lifts and the sky grows bluer over the Taicang village *pailou*, an ornate gateway arch, its pagoda roof curling up toward the sky. The city's name hangs in gold from a sign. We cross the threshold and wander through the cobblestone streets of the town, winding along the stone village wall, painted white and covered in bamboo roofing. My father explains the plan of the village to us—where our family used to live, where the houses and the factories used to be.

In town, the branches of a leafy tree are flounced with hundreds of red ribbons for well wishes. I look, as always, for ferns. I find them in the fissures of the village wall, creeping down the shutters of a home in the longtong through which I can hear the clicking of mahjong tiles. My mother catches on and brings me little plants, and we deliberate: fern or not?

We discover a woman with our surname, a bit younger than my father, who is his cousin, only a little removed. There is a delicate fern, yellow-green, shaped like a hand, under a step in the courtyard of her home. I take it, folding it gently into a piece of paper and into my pocket. She points us in the direction of our family's old house. She says it's being renovated to be turned into a museum, but the workers can let us in if we'd like.

We approach an enormous structure covered with plywood and scaffolding, the past all heaped up. Baba says it must be the family house. We circle it until someone notices us. We explain that we are part of the family that belongs to the house. They happily pry off some plywood and invite us in, telling us *xiaoxin xiaoxin* on our way across the wobbly plank that serves as a walkway across the threshold. I step gingerly onto the narrow piece of wood, one foot in front of the other.

In a few months, everyone here will be locked in their

homes. I won't see my family for two years. My life, like everyone's, will change. We lose control. We scramble and mourn and wait. Within the chaos, I begin to call my brother once per week. An hour at a time. No agenda. At first, it is difficult, getting to know this person. Learning the sound of his voice, what it is like when he is happy, when he is angry, when he is confused or expectant. With time, it grows easier. One day, I come to enjoy it. I begin to miss the weeks without my brother's voice in them.

But now I am in Taicang, looking up into a vault of white plaster and wooden joists carved from an ancient length of tree. Dragons exhale elaborate clouds, phoenixes with waterfall tails wend around the columns. The ceiling is like the belly of a capsized ship. I am transfixed by the scattered details. By how beautiful it is with so much gone. At the end of this room, there is an archway of precise black stone under a bamboo pagoda, also black. Four Chinese characters stand above the head. I don't recognize the characters. It opens into a larger room, and another such gateway.

Mama and Baba and I explore the interlocking space in silence, as if in a cathedral. When we reach the very back room, Baba tells me that when he was small, our entire family would gather here to celebrate the new year. I walk back through our family home, certain on the crooked planks. The shadows against stone, the smell of earth, the ancient light. My parents circle the rooms again and walk together through the gateway, back through each room, whispering, and I'm left for a moment on my own.

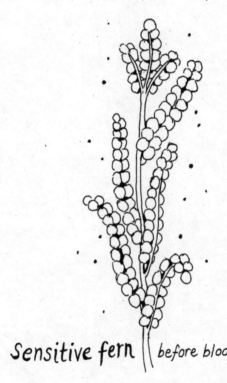

Sensitive fern | before bloom

ACKNOWLEDGMENTS

This memoir would not have been possible without the following people. There aren't enough words or languages for me to adequately express my thanks to:

Jenny Stephens, my agent, for believing in this project and for believing in me.

Jill Meyers, my editor, for your brilliant guidance and for seeing the ghosts in my manuscript.

The wonderful team at A Strange Object and Deep Vellum, for giving my strange object a home.

Emma Hunsinger and Tillie Walden, for illustrating the ferns of my life. For all of the beautiful walks and talking.

Anakwa Dwamena, for your expert fact-checking.

J. Mohorčich, for your attention to style, detail, and voice.

For pushing me up the hill and for making a peaceful home with me.

Rainer Lee, for your companionship on the strange adventure of making a memoir and for reading every draft.

Aries Liao, for giving me a place to safely land each week.

Bess Adler, whose care is evident throughout this book.

Lauren Whitton, for our long friendship.

Mom and Dad, for encouraging me to tell my own story.

Kang, for being my friend.

For the conversations and the support, for making it materially possible for me to make art, for being together: Joy Andrada, Sam Cohen, Hua Hsu, Paul Morello, Abby Farson Pratt, Guion Pratt, Rashida Richardson, Amanda Seda, Jeremy Singer-Vine, Tyler Watson, Jesse Whiles, Asian American Writers Workshop, MacDowell, Millay Arts.

NOTES

Chapter 1
Robbin C. Moran, *A Natural History of Ferns* (Portland, OR: Timber Press, 2009), and John Mickel, *How to Know the Ferns and Fern Allies* (Dubuque, IA: W. C. Brown Co., 1979). Moran's and Mickel's accessible and enthusiastic fern books laid the foundation of botanical knowledge for this book.

Chapter 5
Sarah Whittingham, *Fern Fever: The Story of Pteridomania* (London: Frances Lincoln, 2012).

Chapter 6
Liam Kofi Bright, "White Psychodrama," *Journal of Political Philosophy*, vol. 31, issue 2. Bright's ideas helped me think critically about how I wanted to frame issues of race and identity, especially in narratives about immigration and assimilation.

Chapter 22
Boughton Cobb, Cheryl Lowe, and Elizabeth Farnsworth, *Peterson Field Guide to Ferns: Ferns of Northeastern and Central North America*, 2nd ed. (Boston: Houghton Mifflin, 2005).

Chapter 25
W. G. Sebald, *The Rings of Saturn* (New York: New Directions, 1998). I based my telling of Hong Xiuquan and the Celestial Kingdom (also known as the Taiping Heavenly Kingdom) off Sebald's account.

Chapter 30
Maxine Hong Kingston, *Tripmaster Monkey: His Fake Book* (New York: Knopf, 1989). There are references to "Tripmaster" throughout the book, but Wittman lives in the scene with the saltwater pool.

Chapter 32
Oliver Sacks, *Oaxaca Journal* (Washington, DC: National Geographic, 2002). I am indebted to Sacks's writing, which inspired my own journey to La Chinantla.

Annie Dillard, *For the Time Being* (New York: Knopf, 1999).

ABOUT THE AUTHOR

Wei Tchou's essays and reporting can be found in the *New Yorker*, the *New York Times*, the *Paris Review*, and the *Oxford American*, among other publications. She likes to write about food, nature, and the complications of identity. She is a recipient of a MacDowell Fellowship and has an MFA from Hunter College. She lives in New York City, where she tends a lemon tree.

ABOUT A STRANGE OBJECT

Founded in 2012 in Austin, Texas, A Strange Object champions debuts, daring writing, and striking design across all platforms. The press became part of Deep Vellum in 2019, where it carries on its editorial vision via its eponymous imprint. A Strange Object's titles are distributed by Consortium.